Travelling Light

PUNCH GOES ABROAD

In the same series

THE PUNCH BOOK OF CRICKET
THE PUNCH BOOK OF GOLF
THE PUNCH BOOK OF HEALTH
THE PUNCH BOOK OF SEX AND MARRIAGE

Travelling Light

PUNCH GOES ABROAD

Edited by
Susan Jeffreys

Foreword by
Barry Humphries

A PUNCH BOOK
Published in association with
GRAFTON BOOKS
A Division of the Collins Publishing Group

LONDON GLASGOW
TORONTO SYDNEY AUCKLAND

Grafton Books
A Division of the Collins Publishing Group
8 Grafton Street, London W1X 3LA

Published by Grafton Books 1988

British Library Cataloguing in Publication Data

Travelling light: Punch goes abroad.
1. Voyages and travels——Anecdotes,
facetiae, satire, etc.
I. Jeffreys, Susan   II. Punch
910'.207   G465

ISBN 0-246-13324-4

Printed in Great Britain by Butler & Tanner Ltd,
Frome and London

CONTENTS

LIST OF CARTOONISTS

FOREWORD
by Barry Humphries

Once, long whiles agone, in an attempt to parody certain more extravagant forms of travel writing, I described Budapest as 'the beryl of the Carpathian Basin'. The proprietors of *Punch* have now informed me that I have no legal means of restraining them from reprinting that essay, but they have generously agreed to publish in its stead another of my Hungarian rhapsodies.

I hasten to say that I am not a travel writer; indeed I have the utmost difficulty in scribbling something on a postcard. This is not to say that I don't love travelling, because I do. Fastening seat-belts, inhaling the dubious sub-aroma of humid or gelid refresher towels, reading the safety cards, stealing air sickness bags and recycling them for domestic use, tearing and sundering those innumerable paper and plastic seals which make every airborne snack an obstacle course, all have for me the romance of a page from Hakluyt or a poem by Masefield.

In my youth, in the remote south-east Asian city of Melbourne, travelling meant Overseas. One's friends' parents had been Overseas and had brought back unfocused colour slides and original cast recordings of *My Fair Lady* to prove it. In the Fifties in Australia one almost had the impression that people saved up to go Overseas *especially* to see Rex Harrison and Julie Andrews. There were, of course, lesser attractions which an uncle of mine described during a suburban slide evening as the Trooping of the Guard and the Changing of the Colour. Slide evenings were a popular part of Australian social life in this distant epoch. Calculated to inspire envy and feelings of inferiority in those who had not been Overseas, they were usually of many hours' duration, interrupted by soggy savouries, as each stage of the interminable sea journey from Port Melbourne to Southampton, thence to the Home Counties, Stratford-upon-Avon, Scotland and Wales, was flashed in glorious Kodachrome upon the lounge wall, often upside down. Being Church of England we were generally spared a pictorial tour of Ireland, but all too often, just as we thought our hosts would surely have run out of money, film or both, blurred images of tulips, fjords and snow-capped peaks announced a side trip to the 'clean countries'. A friend of my mother's once told me she was so glad that she and Graham, on their first trip Overseas, had confined their tour to England, Scotland, Holland, Sweden and Switzerland. 'We knew, being Australians, we'd only like the clean countries,' she said nicely.

Now my countrymen, clean or dirty, flock to lands that are unequivocally filthy, and fugitives from filthy countries return the compliment. The Australian dollar has sunk so low the Boat People are flying there. Today there is an invasion of Jumbo People.

But as a means of one-upping the neighbours nothing has quite replaced those venerable slide evenings, for now Everyone has gone Somewhere. I have attended dinner parties where the relative cures for jet lag have been earnestly discussed when the guests have run out of things to say about Acquired Immune Deficiency Syndrome, but it is still just possible to impress those less fortunate than ourselves with airline up-grade stories, since there are still a few people left who have never been bumped up anywhere.

Yet this book is not necessarily for the traveller, for it is sometimes a relief to read about journeys one will never undertake, just as one relishes accounts in the arts supplements of Janacek operas one will never see or hear. When he or she at last puts down this rich and satisfying compendium, the mature armchair traveller should reflect: 'At least I don't have to go *there*.'

Barry Humphries
Cintra, 1988

'*Now, your Lordship, if you wouldn't mind pressing the trigger.*'

Alan Coren

THE GREEN HICKS OF AFRICA

MalaMala, Transvaal, January 13

I walked out of the Jan Smuts departure lounge on the balls of my feet, lightly, towards the plane. The heat came out of the white sky and off the black tarmac, because that is the way it is, out there.

The rest of the party followed me, the birdfaced woman with the Gucci lensbag and the fat man with the polychromatic glasses he kept taking off to see if they were going dark because that is what he paid for them to do and the two fairy Krauts with the big JVC video camera and the tripod and all that stuff with the labels just off that the rich ones have, only they do not have the skill that you have to have or the big JVC is just so much junk, and the Boer with no neck and his wife who had enough neck for two with the little pinched head swivelling on top like a one-man U-boat, and a lot of other people in new safari suits that smelt of Fifth Avenue and Bond Street and the Kurfürstendamm when the heat hit them, and you wondered how they would shape up at their first lion, and you said to yourself I would not want any of these in my corner if the going gets tough.

I was carrying the big Waitrose bag with the rugged Instamatic 110 I always use, and the thick white cream for my head, and the Dr Scholl's arch supports that the wise ones do not go into the bush without, and the heavy duty canisters of Right Guard, and the Dixon's telescope that pulls out into three sections, and *The Big Boy's Book of Animals*

In Colour, and my eyes were flicking back and forth, with that old instinctive flick, the way they have to when there are baggage trucks about, because I have seen what a big baggage truck can do to a man when it charges suddenly out of the sun, and he does not hear it, because the motor makes no sound.

We looked at the plane.

'It has funny things on the front,' said the birdfaced woman.

'They are called propellers,' I said.

'Why are you trembling?' said the bird-faced woman's kid, who had a mouthful of orthodontic girders that sent the sun back in splinters.

'It is the weight of the bag,' I said. 'It is on a nerve on the wrist, and when it is on a nerve on the wrist, your hand trembles. It is a thing you will learn when you are older and have to carry the big bag.'

'It also happens when you have to go on very old planes,' said the woman.

I looked at the woman, but she was looking at her nail.

'I know these planes,' I said. 'These planes are old friends.'

'What sort of a plane is it?' said her son.

'It is a Dakota,' I said. The noon sun is hot in Johannesburg, and makes the mouth go strangely dry, at times. 'They were a very good plane, in the War. In the War, we used to see them a lot.'

'Did you go to the War?' said the son.

I narrowed my eyes against the glare, looking at the rivets on the Dakota's wing. You have to make sure they are all tight before you get on the plane. It is just something you learn.

'I had a good War, small one,' I said. 'But there were times when it was quite bad.'

'He musta been about six in the War,' said the woman, with that Brooklyn twang that makes you think of barmen's towels and dirty cabs. I did not look at her, this time.

'If you had the impetigo in the War,' I said to the kid, 'they put the purple stuff on your face. They took a big bottle with a cod on it, and they shoved white muck in your mouth. You had to be very brave. You had to have *cojones*.'

'What is *cojones*?' asked the kid.

'It is something people talk to take their minds off getting on very old planes,' said his mother.

A uniformed one by the steps cleared his throat.

'Would you mind boarding now, sir?' he said.

'Just a moment, Captain,' I said. The people behind waited. They knew about leadership. 'That tailplane, does it look straight to you?'

The uniformed one looked at the woman.

'He had a bad War,' she said.

We landed at the little Skukuza airstrip, just south of the Kruger National Park, two hours later.

It had been a good flight over the eastern bushveld, and those passengers who had looked out of the window had seen many animals, which is what can happen if you are an inexperienced flier and do not understand that the smart thing to do in an old Dakota is sit rigidly with your eyes shut and not make any sudden movements which could screw up the thing we experienced fliers call the trim.

'We saw lion,' said a small one who helped me off the plane, because something had happened to the nerves in my knees, probably the goddam Waitrose bag again, 'we saw giraffe.'

I smiled that smile at her we old ones have.

'I have seen such things many times, small one,' I said. 'I once got part of an elephant with the Instamatic, from the top of a bus in Regent's Park Road. People will tell you it cannot be done, but if the eye is good and the hand is steady, you can get part of a trunk and even your own thumb. The thing to remember is to squeeze. Never pull.'

She nodded. She would never forget.

We got into the bus after that, and we bounced off down the red-dust track through the scrub and the thorn trees and the torchwood and the Transvaal ebony and the wild date palm and the marula and the tamboti and the giant sourplum and all the other trees in the little book they give you at the airport which all look the same unless you have the little book, and I called out the names as we passed them, only the driver kept correcting me, at the start, but gave up after a while because he could not have been more than about twenty-five, despite all the Head Ranger crap on his shoulder-flashes, and he did not have the book in front of him, and he was beginning to look a fool.

It took an hour to get to the MalaMala Game Reserve, which is a very exclusive game reserve indeed, where the first thing you see as you go through the gate is this little compound of red clay huts with conical thatched roofs.

'Interesting,' I said. 'It is a native kraal, you know.'

They all looked. The driver cut the motor.

'That is the hotel,' he said.

We got out of the bus, and the birdfaced American woman put on the glasses she had round her neck on a diamanté chain and looked at the little huts, hard.

'My God,' she said, 'We're gonna broil in there.'

I laughed that short laugh you laugh when you are an old documentary hand and have seen the thing with Attenborough many times.

'Do not be afraid,' I said, 'those of us who know Africa know that these huts are constructed with great cunning, so that the heat is absorbed by the mud bricks, and drawn up through the thatch by natural exchange.'

The Head Ranger slammed the bus door.

'And if that doesn't work,' he said, 'you switch on the air-conditioner.'

I looked at the shimmering skyline of marula trees, I think, and the vultures or big ducks circling lazily above them. This thing with the Ranger was not going to go away, which is the way it is when two strong men dispute over territory.

We went to our huts, then, and I opened the big Waitrose bag, and I took out the heavy loofah I always carry, and I moved the bed carefully with my foot, and I did not hear the lithe black maid come in to turn down the covers because these people move so silently as to deceive even the keenest ear, and when I knocked over the ice-bucket and fell against the trouser-press, she asked me why I was poking under the divan with the loofah, and I explained to her about snakes, and she ran out of the room, obviously in terror, to judge from her hysterical laughter. Clearly, *The Big Boy's Book of Wild Animals* has not penetrated this far south.

At 4 p.m., we assembled on the verandah to be assigned our Land Rovers for the afternoon trek. I drew the Head Ranger and the birdfaced woman and the two German fags with the big new JVC and the birdfaced woman's kid with the tin teeth, and we walked out across the compound towards the vehicles.

'It does not have sides,' I said. 'It does not have a roof.'

'Good eyes,' said the Head Ranger.

'What happens if an animal tries to jump in?' I said.

The Head Ranger slung himself behind the wheel.

'I go ding-ding,' he said, 'and tell it we're full.'

The kid fell about. The two Krauts clutched one another. The birdfaced woman grabbed the Head Ranger's knee.

'You may not know about Windsor Safari Park,' I said. 'Once a baboon jumped on my Volvo and bent the aerial.'

'Yes,' said the Head Ranger, letting in the clutch, 'I know how he felt.'

We lurched off, out of the compound, down the track, and into the bush, with the Ranger scanning the dust for spoor and his native tracker high on the tailboard watching the bush, and me flicking through *The Big Boy's Book of Wild Animals*, because it is easy to make a mistake when you are either a twenty-five-year-old arrogant pig-headed bloody know-all or a simple black man with hardly more than five languages, and it is important to have a level-headed expert along who can read at a glance that a white rhino weighs five tons and could knock the hell out of a flimsy Land Rover, and who is ready to shriek out this invaluable information whenever there is a risk that you will get close enough for a couple of Kraut pansies to shoot their stupid video, because the smart thing is to take a shot with a well-made British Instamatic 110 from two miles away and then get it enlarged at Boots.

It was around six o'clock, and the sun was a dinner-gong, low, when the intercom crackled on the dash, and one of the other Land Rovers reported a leopard on the other side of the reserve.

'Lucky,' said the Ranger. 'You do not often see leopard.'

'That is because they spring a lot,' I explained. 'They run at sixty miles an hour, and they spring on you. A pity it is getting dark soon and we have to go back, because it would be good to see a leopard.'

'It is the best time to see them,' said the Ranger, hurling the vehicle round and smashing it through the thornbushes. 'It will be hunting.'

'Oh good,' I said.

'Will it be hunting because it is hungry?' said the kid.

'No,' I said, 'it will be hunting just for the fun of it, it is probably full of food, look at all those impala we saw, it has doubtless been tucking in all bloody day, it will not be able to touch another mouthful.'

'Yes,' said the Ranger, 'it will be hunting because it is hungry. They are nocturnal animals. They do not eat during the day.'

I ran my finger down the index, but we were going fast by now, and I could not focus on the eating habits of leopards, and suddenly we splashed across a brown trickle of river, and up the sandy bank, and the native tracker let out a low whistle, and the Ranger braked, and stopped, and cut the engine.

'Please stay absolutely silent,' he said.

I looked where he nodded, and there was this lean assembly of spotted orange haunches and a tail that did not move until you got to the end, and at the end it moved just a little, and it was about thirty yards off, and about thirty yards beyond that there was big kudu buck apparently unaware of its table d'hôte status, and the two Krauts got very excited and unleashed the JVC camera very gently and it began to whirr and the Kraut with the battery-pack told me to stop trembling because it was shaking the camera, and I explained about the Waitrose bag, and he whispered *Was?* so I picked up the big bag to show him, only it was upside down, and the telescope fell on the steel floor of the Land Rover and the big bottle of sun cream for my head smashed and the leopard turned its head so that we could see one yellow eye like a French headlamp, and then it took off.

'See,' I cried, 'sixty miles an hour!'

'You know how much I paid to make this trip?' screamed the birdfaced woman.

Her kid burst out crying, and she hit him with a good left jab, but when she threw the right cross, I think it was meant for me, but I rode it, because you do not lose the old ringcraft.

Nobody talked much on the way back, but the Krauts jabbered a bit and kept glaring at me. They didn't do anything, though, because they had seen I was quick on my feet and they were not going to get into anything they could not get out of.

The native guy on the tailboard just sat there, muttering in one of his damn languages.

When we got back, everybody else sat at one end of the verandah drinking tall drinks, and I sat at the other end at a table with a very old American guy who was reading a two-day-old *Times*. Suddenly, he shoved the paper across, and poked at it with a mottled finger.

'See that?' he said.

I looked.

It said:

> Paris (Reuter)–A new $50,000 annual literary prize aimed at reviving the spirit of adventure and courage which marked the work of Ernest Hemingway is soon to be awarded.

I nodded.

'Waddya think?' he said.

I looked across the dark veld to the orange rim of horizon.

'Easy money,' I said.

23.1.1985

Billy Connolly

THE ELEPHANT MAN

The main drawback in elephant polo is exactly the same as the main drawback in underwater hockey: making people believe that you are actually playing it and not mercilessly extracting the Michael. Elephants, you see, suffer from the same problem as bananas, measles, Spam, Partick Thistle and Hamilton Academicals. They make people snigger before taking them in any way seriously.

The other element that elephant polo shares with underwater hockey, and, of course, uphill ski-ing, is the difficulty that has to be endured just travelling to the game. In the case of elephant polo, the only officially marked-out pitch happens to be in

Nepal, at a place called Tiger Tops, seven hours' drive from Kathmandu. The flight from Heathrow – jumbo jet, naturally – went by Kuwait, Dubai and on to Delhi, the interminable flying hours bringing the usual loss of sleep, loss of appetite, loss of interest, and, inevitably at Delhi, loss of baggage, leading to a sudden loss of the will to live.

At Heathrow, I was met by my fellow team members, Ringo Starr and Barbara Bach. We were to be joined at Dubai by a fourth member, and together we would represent Cartier the jewellers. Who else? My heart danced a wild jig in my breast when I learned that Barbara Bach had never been closer to an elephant than sitting in the audience at the circus, and that Ringo's sole experience was a sixpenny ride at the zoo, side-saddle on one of those bench-type sets. Ringo also confided that he played all stick games left-handed, which made him a natural right-winger if the game was to be played anything like football. My airline ticket bore the legend: VIP FAMOUS COMED.

The journey was a bit tiring and came to an end at Kathmandu, where we spent the night in, believe it or not, the Yak & Yeti Hotel, which boasted, among other things, Yetiburgers on the menu. Poor Yeti, no wonder he keeps himself so well hidden. Apart from the normal Do Not Disturb signs, shampoo and shower cap, each guest is supplied with a little cardboard Yeti footprint, on which is printed 'Clean My Shoes Please'. Oh, how are the mighty fallen. I wonder if he keeps in touch with Nessie, who shares just about the same fate.

In the morning, we set off on the seven-hour journey through the Himalayan foothills, across the fertile plain and thus to the jungle, where we received instructions on survival: 'Empty your shoes in the morning before putting them on – scorpion stings can be nasty.' Also, 'When confronted by a tiger, don't look it straight in the eye, the tiger will interpret this as a challenge.' Fat chance, I wonder how a tiger interprets a backside disappearing into the distance at a great rate of knots?

For elephant polo, the rules were described thus: 'The rules are basically the same as in horsey polo; make believe you are on the motorway and mustn't cross the central reservation.' This left us slightly more bewildered about the game than we were back at Heathrow, but gave us something to think about as we lay in bed at night, listening to the jungle noises of various species of animals, slinky, cuddly, scaly, many-legged and many-toothed, treating each other like fast food outlets. No wonder some of them are endangered, they keep eating one another. The hotel even laid on the ultimate voyeuristic diversion, a staked-out oxen being killed by a wild tiger.

The elephant is a lovely, big, friendly beastie. Its main fault, leading to its domination by quite awful little people who prod and bash it with instruments that would get you jailed in Glasgow for mere ownership, is its total unawareness of its own size. It thinks that it is about the same size as a Border collie, and behaves accordingly.

There isn't any reason why it should be the colour it is – it doesn't need to blend into the background when it has no natural enemies, except, that is, for the awful little people who take great pleasure in prodding it with awful things. It could quite happily go through life covered in Royal Stuart tartan, or Paisley pattern, or even green corduroy, just like the elephant so adored by my daughter. Come to think of it, elephants would probably get round to discovering that green corduroy was excellent stuff for hiding in the jungle, and leaping out and stamping on, therefore stamping out, awful little people with horrible proddy things.

The clothing deemed *de rigueur* for this exotic pastime consists of brown riding boots, white breeches, team shirt and wally hat or topi. There is also the polo mallet with extremely long shaft. The teams of four players line up facing each other and try by one means or another to prod, whack, shove and harry a ball, not much bigger than a cricket ball, into a goal about ten feet wide. It's a bit like sitting astride a single-decker bus and prodding an orange around Piccadilly Circus with a billiard cue.

It is infuriating, exasperating, swear-word inducing in the extreme, but above all, it is great fun. The most spectacular team was The Oberoi Ladies, four very attractive American girls who look after ageing Asian elephants in Kathmandu, and play extremely well, and look absolutely splendid in their outfits. Soldiers do like dressing up, don't they?

The Scotland team contained two English-sounding Scots, an Irishman, and a fellow whose surname suggests an ancestry very far from Edinburgh. A noisy lot. King Mahendra's Trust team wore raincoats and played brilliantly. British Airways, led by a Concorde captain, contained Olympic stan-dard horsey people who played the game as it was intended. There were also two teams from Tiger Tops, who own all the elephants and mahouts. 'Mahout' is the local word for 'awful little person who hits and prods elephant with instruments generally reserved for poking the fires of Hull'.

The World Championship was won by Tiger Tops Tuskers, who, most unfairly, speak fluent Jumbo. Cartier, of whose team I was a fully paid-up member, came in a creditable last, and collected tiger-pawmark ashtrays for their trouble.

The game is great if treated as a good laugh, awful if treated seriously. If football is a gentleman's game played by ruffians, and if rugger is a ruffian's game played by gentlemen, then elephant polo is a Hooray Henry's game played by Herberts.

5.1.1986

'You're not far out! Actually we're descended from the crew of a unit making a re-make of a film about the Bounty*!'*

TROUBLE
ON T'SAFARI

*ALBERT joins a package holiday to
Africa*

*'It's amazing what our Mr
Tribley can do with a swamp-
lizard!'*

'You're supposed to haggle!'

'Normally we like to be a little further by the third week!'

'No, I must admit that left to ourselves we'd probably never invent the ethnic joke.'

'You know what burns me up? Having to wait sixty seconds for the darn picture.'

Robert Morley

THE ONE-UP, ROUND-THE-WORLD GOURMET

He sat beside me at the bar and, when I enquired idly about his plans, he announced he was off to Strasbourg to eat a goose. So many travellers attempt too much. His reply encapsulated a singleness of purpose altogether admirable. I don't now remember to whom I was talking, only that it was in Buck's, where such affirmations are – or at least were – listened to without distress.

How far is one prepared to go for a good meal?

I posed the question to several acquaintances. A number demanded elaboration: Do you mean a free good meal? How good is good? Myself, I would be prepared to go a long way, but then, of course, I like travelling, let alone food. Clutching my Michelin, how often have I sought out the rosette and crossed spoons and demanded the speciality of the house and, strangely enough, how often have I been disappointed.

There is a *Café de Paris* in Biarritz which serves, for a few golden weeks of the year, a sort of special white truffle with apples, which I found as nasty as tripe and couldn't finish. The baby lamb at *Les Beaux* is, to my mind, altogether too babyish – a veritable slaughter of the innocents. Reminding me of a celebrated restaurateur in Gerard Street – now, alas, retired – who would explain the ritual murder necessary to prepare the feast he had in store for me. 'Mr Morley, you take a baby frog just as he utters his first bellow,

and cut off his head. You must do it in the moonlight, otherwise it is no use, and then you throw away everything but the tip of the heart where the coralete is' (there was always, in the description, a word I could not catch) 'then, later, you bake this for a dozen hours on a slow peat fire, turning it over and over, and then you butter it at the table.'

'If you want a really first-class moussaka,' I heard myself announce the other day, 'you'll have to go to Newbury.' The fellow who was unlucky enough to be within earshot hadn't even mentioned moussaka and, as far as I know, never touched the stuff.

We each have a Gourmet Guide hidden on our person and long to expose it. 'Don't be put off by the Formica tabletops,' we urge each other, 'the chef used to cook for Onassis before he took to the bottle.' We are speaking of the former chef, naturally – for we all know, Aristotle is teetotal.

The impression we seek to leave is of a blue tit which has already skimmed the cream. When the milk-bottle is taken inside it will not be the same. The eateries we extol today will, tomorrow, be ruined by the hoi-polloi – places we would not be seen dead in. 'Not quite what it was, is it?' we enquire of the still-faithful customer. 'I hear the *ptarmigan à la façon de Président Giscard* is precooked and frozen.' Once the hat-check girl and the diners' club take over we are off, once more, in search of the little restaurant in Shrewsbury where the firemen eat because the captain's wife comes from Bayonne and does a mincemeat tart which is out of this world.

I have two distinct approaches when eating out. Quiet confidence, as host – a hint of formality in my manner of greeting the staff. I try to impart a sense of occasion to the ritual of seating my guest and choosing the food and wine, adding a touch of originality by asking for the salt to be taken away until we have need of it. 'I don't know if you feel as I do,' I remark to my friend, 'but I cannot bear a cruet with the aperitif.' The use of the word *cruet*, here, is, I flatter myself, not without courage. Occasionally, before ordering the meal, I will summon a waiter and enquire about his wife. 'Better, I hope?' I tell him. I don't actually know whether the fellow has a wife but he will not care to correct me, though he may look a little puzzled – but I am confident that my companion will mistake his bewilderment for gratitude. The impression I wish to give – and, I have no doubt, succeed in giving – is that of the late Noël Coward in charge of a happy ship: the crew's troubles are my troubles – up to a point, of course. Before choosing the wine, I always say quite simply and, indeed, truthfully, that I know nothing whatever about it. When the others have suitably expressed their disbelief, I suggest we take the wine-waiter's advice. 'Something you want to get rid of,' I tell him encouragingly. 'Perhaps a Sancerre 1958, or Sauvigny de Clos Montard '49?' I usually give a little chuckle as he departs. When he returns with the bottle I am careful not to taste it – this is a privilege I reserve for my guest.

When our roles are reversed, of course I am a totally different creature. I go for the overkill. 'What a delightful bistro!' I exclaim. 'Blue beams! I don't think I've ever seen blue beams before *and* brown paper napkins! So convenient for the Natural History Museum – it's just round the corner, surely? How did you find it? Let's stick to the set meal, shall we? It's sure to be excellent ... I'll have what you're drinking – half a carafe will be ample. How long has this place been going? ... And I've never heard of it. What do you suppose they're having at the next table? Who would you say the people who come here are, mostly? ... Students? It's so jolly and unpretentious. I am reminded of a little place half-way up the Bosporus on the right-hand side – you know it, of course – I was taken there by our Ambassador to eat yoghourt, and then we discovered this perfectly marvellous way they cook kid – in a blanket. You must try it next time you're there; just mention my name – or even the Ambassador's.'

Stored among the disorder of my memory is a positive armoury of food bombs to demolish the culinary oneupmanship of others. I always insist, for instance, that the *millefeuilles* at the *Château de Madrid* is worth negotiating the hairpin-bends of the Grand Corniche. 'I don't know why being circular should make all the difference,' I tell anyone who is listening, 'but somehow it does. Kobe beef in Tokyo is best, really, at the Hilton. They seem to have a particularly skilled masseur. You know that the Japanese massage the beasts on the hoof? I can't think why we don't do it here.'

No experience is too horrific to go into my book and be subsequently translated into a trap for the unwary.

The journey up-country from Bangkok to the Temple of Divine Light is seldom undertaken by train – at any rate by tourists, who prefer the river-steamer, or bus. I, on the other hand, went by rail, and have never forgotten the breakfast. I can still taste the cold fried egg, nestling in sago and topped with Soy sauce. 'Worth all the boredom of the Jade Buddha,' I maintain, stoutly. 'Be sure and catch the nine-twenty, and insist on the restaurant-car.'

One of the legends of travel I like to retell to anyone thinking of returning from Australia by air and re-fuelling in Teheran, is that if they hasten to the Transit Lounge and take the small door on the left, next to the gentlemen's lavatory, they will find themselves at the back of the Imperial Caviare Emporium, where they have only to rouse the attendant, who sleeps under the counter, to secure enormous quantities of sturgeon roe at knock-down prices.

It may well be that the store exists, but I have not, after numerous attempts, ever discovered it. I am not sure I want to. It gives me something to look forward to on the flight.

How dull the world would be if we all knew the mystery of Glamis Castle – which reminds me of a little teashop on the left as you leave the Keep, where they serve a really excellent Scotch pancake.

22.1.1975

Barry Humphries

HUNGARIAN GHOULISH

A notorious sodomite always leaps to mind whenever I travel by Lot, the Polish airline. The Hungarian carrier Malev is somehow more suggestive of *Star Wars* or an equivocal creature from a romance of science fiction.

It was Malev who recently lifted me out of Vienna on the comfortable half-hour hop up the Danube to Budapest. During the flight attractive hostesses dispensed chocolates and fermented plum juice to the passengers, who included impeccably dressed black businessmen from Lagos and Iraq with Samsonite briefcases and digital watches, and a sprinkling of trade union delegates, conference-bound.

In the posh hotels of Budapest, everyone who is not Hungarian looks like a trade union delegate, ogling utopia. Taxi-ing across the tarmac of East European aerodromes is a bumpier and more invigorating ride than most western travellers are accustomed to expect and Budapest is no exception, but once inside the terminal – which smells excitingly of Balkan tobacco and petroleum – the tourist whose visa is in order finds himself quickly re-united with his sponge bag.

I changed some money into the red-cabbage coloured currency of Hungary and caught a taxi to town. A version of the Union Jack (was one of the stripes too narrow – a cross the wrong colour?) rippled from lamp-posts along my route to the hotel, and I discovered later that a senior member of the British Government was also paying a visit to Budapest later the same day. My assumption had at first been that a Union Jack was as close as the hospitable Hungarian authorities could get to the Australian ensign.

We stopped at some lights and my driver bought a newspaper. The newspaper. Only four pages long. This was palpably that miracle of condensation which Fleet Street, with the help of the unions, has yet to achieve.

On a roadside construction site the immense reinforced concrete shell of a building in progress betrayed signs of long exposure to the elements. With the Union Jack fluttering nearby, there was something irresistibly and reassuringly British about those mossy girders and weed-fronded parapets along which men with buckets crept as though they had been offered rich incentives for never completing their tasks.

The two 'best' hotels in Budapest are the Hilton (built around a thirteenth-century Dominican cloister) on Castle Hill in Buda, and the Intercontinental in Pest, right on the

Danube. Since Western movie companies are constantly shooting 'period' epics in and around Budapest, these two hotels frequently accommodate those legendary beings, the fops and featherbrains of filmdom. Stories abound of their fabulous deeds, their infantile extravagances and gross intemperance. No state in the Communist bloc misses its aristocracy more than Hungary, so the exotic inhabitants of the grand hotels are a constant source of wonder and delight.

I always like to stay at the Gellért Hotel on the Buda side by the old chain bridge. Its opulent limestone facade looks up the khaki Danube as it did before the Second World War, though the interior has been refurbished in that bleak Fifties style deemed up-to-date in Eastern Europe, all cream, green and maroon, with Blondwood veneer furniture. Somehow this nondescript mode of interior decoration, installed to cheer up Western tourists, is infinitely more oppressive than the overstuffed mahogany gloom, the sumptuous seediness we long to discover in those few old hotels which have survived war and cultural revolution.

On the night I arrived the excellent dining room was almost deserted except, of course, for the gypsy band which proceeded to give me its undivided musical attention. My requests were solicited, but the poignant airs from forgotten Austro-Hungarian operettas which I hummed to the chief fiddler seemed to confound his powers of recollection, so that my *hors d'oeuvre* of goose liver was devoured to the accompaniment of *The Way We Were*. Nevertheless I tipped the band in various foreign currencies throughout my solitary meal, and as the attentive waiter brought me a delectable *fogos* fish from Lake Ballaton, garnished with an emulsion flecked with dill, the five-piece orchestra relapsed into their voluptuous repertoire of Zigeuner melodies. Music is one of the special enchantments of a Hungarian holiday, and you can fling open your hotel windows at any hour of the night and hear, wafted seemingly across the Danube, the curdled harmonies of the *czardas*.

There are not many hotels I know where the guests, having donned bathrobes and slippers, may descend by lift to a vast and rambling thermal underworld where almost every known form of hydrotherapy is available for little more than a pound. At Rotorua in New Zealand, where the earth's crust resembles *millefeuilles*, the ailing and obese patrons of Brent's Hotel 'take the muds' at an adjacent clinic, and I have stayed at a modern conference centre in Palm Springs which incorporates a fitness club and spa on a sacred site where redskins once pow-wowed underwater. But the Gellért Hotel, with its subterranean labyrinth of mineral treatment amenities, is the most mysterious and the most attractive.

Unless you know the Carpathian Basin well, you probably do not think of Budapest as a thermal zone with at least nine medicinal bathing establishments which have been going strong since the Turkish occupation, yet the Hungarian capital is a haven where galvano-therapy and gingival massage are constantly requested *and dispensed*.

Pride of the Gellért is its cavernous Roman bath decorated at the turn of the century in the Byzantine style. It resembles a swamped mosque, dimly lit, where a large congregation of devout hydrophiliacs shuffle, loll and paddle in their tepid element, beneath a steamy vault of azure mosaic.

There are many surprises in store for the tourist exploring its dusky anterooms. In one humid chamber I came upon a scene rather like one of Gustave Doré's graphic illustrations to Dante's *Inferno*. A group of elderly loin-clothed patrons were suspended by rubber neck braces over a sombre and sulphurous abyss. No doubt they were voluntarily undergoing treatment for some disorder of the vertebrae, since they uttered no sighs or exclamations of protest as they dangled there in the vaporous gloom, even if the strangeness of that vision suggested punishment rather than cure.

Elsewhere I discovered a warren of massage cubicles where the art of a contemporary master of the macabre, Francis Bacon, was vividly evoked. Flabby, veal-coloured men were sprawled and in some cases *draped* in folds and swags of cellulite over marble slabs where they were violently attacked by youths wielding enormous, soap-laden shaving brushes. Once they had been enveloped in suds they were slapped and pummelled with what appeared to be miniature cricket bats, until the tiles echoed with the sound of willow on lather.

In summer, guests may sunbathe nude on the roof of the hotel, overlooking panoramic views of the city, and behind the Gellért, a leafy hillside studded with pumpkin and pimento villas, once the houses of the rich and now diplomatic residences. The hotel also boasts a swimming-pool with a mechanical wave-making machine, one of the few I know to exist anywhere in the world (not forgetting, of course, the similar device at the municipal baths at the Elephant and Castle, Southwark).

Some of the best walks are on Castle Hill, the area around the former royal castle on a narrow plateau above the Danube. The old Renaissance, Gothic and Baroque houses have been artfully reconstructed since the War, and at number 8 Országház Utca is an antiquarian bookshop (open afternoons only) with an interesting selection of English volumes. I have always liked to browse along the shelves devoted to English books in foreign secondhand bookshops. One finds all those holiday authors left behind years ago in hotel bedrooms. Michael Arlen, Cecil Roberts, Hall Caine, Dornford Yates, Warwick Deeping, Guy Thorne and Ian Hay. In this dusty old bookshop, which I am told is still privately owned, I have never failed to discover an edition of Starkie's *Raggle-Taggle*, that classic description of a Balkan journey undertaken in a happier epoch than our own.

In the same building is the honey and honeycake shop run by the National Apiary Co-operative. Here many varieties of excellent and inexpensive honeycakes may be bought. For the best gourmet food in Budapest you should visit Vörös Csillag, a hotel restaurant on Freedom Hill with a pleasant terrace, or Vadrózsa, at Pentelei Molnár Utca 15. (NB. Open Thursday and Friday for dinner and Saturday for lunch and dinner.) This is one of the few private restaurants in the city and it is in the garden of a private villa. That local delicacy, goose liver, is here priced higher on the menu than caviar.

The opera in Budapest costs little more than a pound and concerts are also one of the city's most attractive bargains. Interesting, too, are the antique shops, but it is possible to have one's purchases seized by a Customs officer at the station or airport, where the vigilant authorities love nothing more than to repossess art treasures whether they be rare ikons or lustre-ware bookends.

In Hungary it is unwise to buy anything which could be remotely construed as an *objet d'art*. Cases are not unknown where a confiscated vase has turned up in a Budapest antique shop a week later, ready for recycling.

Foreigners with a justifiable fear of Communist red tape are, however, agreeably surprised by the speedy formalities attending their departure from Hungary, unless they are detained at the souvenir shop where the best buys are the bags of paprika in varying strengths and the potent apricot brandy, or *Barack Palinka*.

That said, readers would be ill-advised to fly to Budapest or any other Eastern European port solely to avail themselves of the duty-free shopping facilities.

21.1.1981

Miles Kington

IN SEARCH OF LENIN

Monday the 29th

The Russians have no god, but they have Lenin. His Old Testament face glares out from walls, banners, postcards, books, postage stamps. His vision of heaven on earth is still gospel in the second most powerful country in the world, and his writings are its scriptures. He is the only man I know of who is still lying in state fifty years after his death and breaking attendance figures. He is Queen Victoria, Churchill, Wellington, Cromwell rolled into one, with something to spare. It may be because he is so precious to the Russians that he is the one great attraction *not* forced on the tourists. I am not a religious man, at least not about religion, but I suddenly wanted to find out about Lenin worship.

I especially wanted to see how they dealt with their one great problem.

At the time of the Revolution Lenin was almost fifty and had only another half dozen years to live. It was really the first time in his life he had not been in exile, in prison or harried about Europe. So it stood to reason that there couldn't be much left of the man's belongings to put on show, with which to bolster the Lenin worship which seems to have replaced religion in the Soviet Union. Put another way, what on earth was there in all the Lenin museums round Russia and more precisely in the huge Lenin Museum off Red Square, before which we now stood?

I examined the first exhibit, a notice board outside the door.

'Open at eleven,' I said eventually. (I had been learning Russian for a month.) 'But not on Mondays,' I added shortly.

So we went to Lenin's tomb. There was no queue.

'Closed,' I translated.

So we went into St Basil's Cathedral to study Tsarist art and to the Pushkin Museum to see the Impressionists and Picassos, and home to reflect that they weren't exactly shoving Communist culture down our throats but that we weren't beaten yet.

Tuesday the 30th

Tuesday was worse.

The Lenin Museum was closed. Lenin's Tomb was closed. The History Museum was closed. Still, the Intourist office was open.

'I'm sorry,' said the girl. 'Lenin Museum is always closed on the 30th day of the month. Lenin's tomb is shut until April for reconstruction. But you can see Tsarist art in St Basil's Cathedral or French Impressionists at . . .'

I played my trump card.

'What about Lenin's country house?'

She consulted guides.

'It is closed on Tuesdays.'

'Tomorrow?'

'Also on thirty-first day of each month.'

So we went to see the pre-revolutionary riches in the Kremlin and then to see an opera at the Bolshoi. It was Rimsky-Korsakov's *The Tsar's Bride*. What do the Russians think they are playing at? Are they serious about Communism or aren't they? Round two to them.

Wednesday the 31st

On the usual list of things that people hold against Moscow are: the way churches are closed down or only frequented by a few old people, the way tourists can buy quality stuff in duty-free shops that the natives can't get so cheap, the way big blocks of flats are flung up, the way massive official sculptures are forced on the populace. True, but all this is equally true of London. I liked Moscow. There are no traffic jams; public transport is efficient. The streets are wide, so is the skyline, the eyes can breathe. They preserve old buildings and care for the vistas. There are trees and little parks everywhere. The men have fine faces. Above all, the Lenin Museum is open on Wednesdays!

Before I went to Moscow I knew two things about Lenin. One, it wasn't his real name. Two, he couldn't possibly be forty feet high with a fist permanently clenched in the air, as his pictures and statues tended to suggest. In other words, I knew nothing about Lenin, which I rectified on Monday the 29th with a biography of him in English, from which emerged the curious fact that there were at least two Lenins. One was the public Lenin who strove heroically all his life to organise, preach, think, write and act, who has ended up as the forty-foot monster with the clenched fist. The other was the private Lenin, a man of huge charm and ease, invariably described as magnetic or vital, with a bottomless fund of humour. I had expected most things, but not to find that Lenin had been great fun to be with.

The Lenin Museum celebrates the public man, of course. It's full of writings and books, details of workers' Soviets, pictures of revolutionary heroes, models of the British Museum Reading Room with one seat marked Lenin and another marked Marx. But because there simply isn't enough of the public Lenin left to fill the place, you get the private man as well, and you suddenly realise that you hadn't seen him *smiling* before. He looked quite different. There's one superb photograph of him playing chess with Gorki in Capri, another of him in an old hat walking in the hills, and the Lenin there is a real person, an exceedingly attractive person, the man who hated being lionised and adulated and given heroic status.

What would *he* have thought of the Lenin Museum?

Upstairs, every hour, they show a film of Lenin's life. Much of it is cobbled together from tiny scraps of newsreel, often edited and repeated to blow a five second fragment up into a thirty second sequence. (The film used to be twenty minutes long – it has been recently stretched to thirty. . . .) But there is one long genuine scene of him strolling and chatting in the Kremlin with a colleague, and it was impossible to watch it and not feel that here was a genuinely good and great man. Impossible to explain, too.

What was strange was that I was being drawn towards the man for reasons which the Russians would no doubt find frivolous; certainly for things which they did not feel it worth emphasising. It's not hard to make fun of the over-serious Lenin cult, in the same way that it's easy to make fun of the austere side of Russian life, the drabness of shops, the sameness of clothes. But there's something else there as well. Why should there be as many postcards with flowers on for sale as political postcards? Why should the supposedly inhuman modern Russian art at the Tretyakov Gallery turn out to be incredibly varied and often delicate (and a great relief after the Western avant-garde)? Why does no-one ever notice how many patches of trees and green there are in Moscow? An inveterate traveller of my acquaintance told me on my return: 'The Russians are basically among the most humane of people.' Good for a laugh? But I know what he means.

Thursday the 1st

No, I am not now nor ever have been a Communist. Yes, this is getting a bit serious. Yes, Lenin's home is open on Thursdays. It's 25 miles out of Moscow and a fine place to be when, as today, it's −20° Centigrade and the snow is falling absent-mindedly on the woods around the house.

'Not many people ask to come out here,' says our Intourist guide.

More fool them. Lenin's home was a cluster of small nineteenth century classical buildings, something like American colonial style classical. It was difficult to keep the biggest house heated properly, so they tended to move across to the small house in winter. They being his brothers and sisters and wife and nephews, because he was a great family man, and although the authorities have had a bash at stressing the presence of a forty-foot hero with clenched fist, it was a losing battle. What you remember is the bench he sat on in the garden, the room where he showed films to the villagers, the elegance of the simple furniture, his favourite long walk in the woods. In his last years he was increasingly incapacitated, partly because he worked himself to death and partly because of a near-assassination (he died with one bullet still in him, years later), which explains the extra hand-rails on the banisters and the extraordinary Rolls-Royce in the garage, caterpillar tracks at the rear, skis in front.

Now, if I were in charge of Lenin worship in Russia, this house would present me with a problem. There, Lenin becomes real, which means that he becomes unreal as the bronze official statue and the enormous face on the banner. It's dangerous to bring a deity down to human scale. 'Not many people ask to come out here.' I wonder how many are encouraged. The few tourists there with us were all foreigners. If I were in charge of Lenin worship, of course, I would say that my search for the real Lenin is bourgeois Western sentimentality – that even if this little house contains more genuine relics of Lenin than all the spacious halls of the Museum, the Museum is more accurate because it represents what he said and what he did.

And yet I like to think that Lenin too would half agree with me. Right to the end of his life he hated bureaucracy and red tape. He demanded quick decisions, insisted that officials keep in touch with facts and with people. Before he died he recommended that Stalin be dismissed, because he was arrogant, conceited and too contemptuous of those below him. That sort of Lenin might be difficult to accommodate today. He is worshipped, yes, but remember what they

'Let's go to Russia before it gets spoilt.'

always say about any god – if he came back today, who would recognise him? Would the faceless bureaucrats, the solemn power-mongers, really want the real Lenin back? No, it's safer to give him a permanent clenched frown and make him forty foot high. If you put his body on show in his tomb, and parade his writings in his museums, and reprint his books in all languages, you can persuade people that Lenin never really died, that he is still with us. Which helps to disguise the uncomfortable fact that since he died in 1924 there has been nobody to replace him.

14.2.1973

'*. . . this is your Captain Boris Stupkov speaking . . . welcome aboard Aeroflot flight twenty-three . . . we are flying quite high, very quick and somewhere over the Soviet Union . . . thank you . . .*'

GETTING THERE

*'Be patient, darling Daddy's just waiting
to see who picks up the very last case . . .'*

*'Colonel Tribble, stop weighing yourself
and start exploring.'*

*'Letting him come was
the only way I could get him
to put up the money to
pay for all this.'*

Stanley Reynolds

DOWN AND OUT IN PARIS, ILLINOIS

Travelling across America, by car or bus or train, is one of the genuine pleasures left in the world. It is, indeed, the thing all Americans do themselves or at least dream of doing, but when they decide to head West or go back East or up North or down South they do not get the really fine treatment that a foreigner gets. The reason for this is simple. The South still hates the Yankees because of the Civil War, which the Southerners refuse even to call the Civil War, calling it the War Between the States instead. And Westerners think the United States ends at the Hudson River and Easterners, such as myself, think they are all hicks out there west of the Hudson. New Yorkers, who don't really go anywhere ever, are the worst offenders. They think anything north of New York is Bridgeport. Bridgeport, Connecticut, is the Watford Gap of America.

Untainted by any of this regional squabbling, the foreign tourist is very welcome and the British traveller most of all because he speaks English real good, for a foreigner. The new low-cost flights have brought a bumper crop of British tourists to America and I reckon they will go on receiving the A treatment until that unhappy day when Scotland or West Ham play in California and their massed supporters march down Route 66.

I have some little experience of the way a visiting foreigner is grasped to the American bosom for I once drove West in a Volkswagen with Rhode Island number plates. Now, Rhode Island is the smallest state in the Union and is often overlooked when people sit around bars and try to name all the 50 states for a bet – when the bars are opened all day, time sometimes hangs heavy. Still, Rhode Island is a part of the United States, in fact it is the first state because it declared itself free of the British Yoke on May 4, 1776, two months before the rest, but I didn't seem able to convince the Western hayseeds of this. VWs were also a rare sight then and that might have helped their ignorance along.

'You speak real good,' one of them said to me after he noticed the Rhode Island plates. 'Let me buy you a drink.'

I let him buy me several. And I got myself into one of those embarrassing situations where I couldn't suddenly tell him he was very ignorant and that I was clearly not some kind of a Greek but one of his own. He would have thought I was a city slicker from back East working a con on him. It might prove dangerous. But it was wondrous listening to him and seeing how proud he was of the twelve miles of paved road in his home town and how natural he thought it was for me to come out all the way from Greece to see the marvel of it for myself. His father was named Homer and he had an older brother named Homer too and everybody knew Homer had been some kind of a famous goddamn old-time Greek and, well, put it there and have another.

Well, maybe that is cliché America. But there is a hidden America out there that is vanishing a little bit more each year and is well worth seeing before it is lost forever. Of course most British TV viewers think they know all about America because they've seen *Dallas* and *Charlie's Angels* but it isn't like that at all. Certainly there is skyscraper America and there are beaches full of silver sand and beaches with golden sand and suburbs with tree-shaded streets so cosy you'd think you were in an old Fred McMurray movie. And all very nice it is, and yet there is this other and swiftly vanishing

America out there as well but the travel writers never seem to tell us about it.

It is Jack Kerouac America, Carl Sandburg America, Sinclair Lewis America, Jack London America, Walt Whitman America and, I suppose, to carry out the literary lineage, Sam Clemens America too. It is the America of the open road, of the hitch-hiker and the hopper of freight trains. I had quite thought they were lost forever until a year ago when I found myself in Iowa. It was some woebegone town, plain as coffee grounds, a city of hardware stores and lunch-counters with steamy plate-glass windows, men in lumberjack shirts standing talking on street corners, talking in big, deep but quiet voices, voices redolent of pioneer days before someone decided everybody in America should talk through their noses. There was, as in all these towns, the old-fashioned hotel and I knew just what it would be like in that hotel's lobby; full of ghosts it would be, the shades of old-time travelling salesmen, drummers, swapping lies under the ornate chandeliers. No doubt the hotel would have the old brass spittoons stored away somewhere.

The brochures will tell you all about all the *nice* places you can get to very cheaply nowadays but they don't do travel posters and guided tours of the tacky lunch-counters or the now (practically) defunct hobo jungles down by the railroad tracks with the broken bottles in the long grass.

Well, who'd want to do the Woody Guthrie Hobo Tour or the Jack Kerouac Wino Back-Alley Package Holiday, anyway? I would. And all my friends. Because this is the myth-making part of America. And, too, there is time enough to sit in the grand hotel when you are old and grey and grateful for the five star service. To go to New York and not see Harlem, to go to Philadelphia and not spend a night in one of those seedy dim-lighted, heavy with menace bars full of hookers and pimps in the City of Brotherly Love, to ignore downtown St Louis, pool-room Denver, Burke's Hotel in Marquette, Iowa, St Mary's Street in San Antonio, Baltimore Street in Baltimore, Blackburn Avenue in Portland, Oregon, or a sailor's Saturday night out in San Diego ... why it's like going to Brazil and never seeing the jungle!

This is not Ma and Pa America and it's not Mum and Dad's notion of a trip to America. But I love those comfortable old hotels, like the Palmer House in Chicago, on Wabash Avenue and State Street, now the forgotten part of modern Chicago, but the hotel where the robber barons sat up all night chewing on big black cigars and chewing up the map of the United States, parcelling out the country to one another just like they owned it, which, of course, they did. And up the street, at the corner of State and Lake, with Lake Michigan howling up the street, where the wind gets so bad in the winter time that they have sometimes to stretch a length of rope across the street so you can hang on and not get blown away, there is a marvellous, brown-stained, old-fashioned greasy spoon and bar and grill, with a good-looking waitress, chewing gum and looking as I-Seen-It-All-But-I-Ain't-Broken-Not-Yet-At-Least as Ann Sheridan, taking your order saying, 'Listen, fella, where'd you pick up that accent?'

'London, England.'

'Listen,' says a John Garfield sort of fellow standing at the bar, 'I was stationed right outside of London, England, during the war. Sure I was,' he says, 'Wigan, right outside Liverpool, right outside London, England. Listen,' he says, 'what'll you have?'

That was last year. Maybe I should book right away, right now, before I get any older and have to stay at the Hilton.

21.1.1981

'How are we goin' to manage, Mum, about packing these here clogs?'

'You'll soon find getting their lips stuck to the tap is an occupational hazard.'

Stephen Potter

THE ABOMINABLE SKI-MAN

Is it my children or my great-grandchildren who ask me, nowadays, to give some guidance on winter sportsmanship? The mind gets confused. But it is certain that I did, in 1925, have that fortnight on the nursery slopes at Pontresina; and that perhaps is why they crowd round me now, constantly asking, probing. Over that distance of time, the sowing of the smallest seed may bring forth something to sustain the modern way of ski life.

'And did you actually climb up the hills yourself, in those days?' said little Sarah, a descendant.

'What, every step?' said the maturer voice of Annabel, an elderly grandchild.

'No ski-lifts at all?' said a two-year-old.

'One, at St Moritz.'

'You must be exaggerating,' said V., a typical daughter-in-law. I was, but I was simplifying it for them. 'As you climb near the top, as the air becomes more rarefied, anoxia sets in, and you had to wait between each step to get your breath. It was like this: – 'Step – gasp, gasp, gasp. Step,' and so on I repeated. Children remember that sort of thing all their lives.

Soon some of the older generation were asking me questions.

'What sort of equipment do you think we ought to have?'

'Well, of course in all these basic situations it's got to be one thing or the other. Tremendously up to date – '

'Seven clip boot sort of thing?'

'What? Yes, or the opposite. Stuff which looks tremendously well used. You might for instance take *our* old rig,' I said, using a slang word of 1895.

'You used to tie your skis on with some kind of thong, didn't you?' said Jimmy, a grand-stepson. 'Those were the days when you used to turn by crossing one ski over another. Extraordinary.'

'Not necessarily,' I said.

It was agreed that equipment must not be overdone. In other words only an international should appear with more than one pair of skis: although the rest of us, with the aid of our Handbook, should be able to talk quite fluently about the varying OK-ness of split, one-piece, or cracked-edge construction.

Nor should we be covered with badges. Wear just one, if it happens to mean something ('The Down-hill Club,' I think one of them said. Or were they pulling my leg?)

When approaching ski resorts by air, it is best to look as little like a mountaineer as possible. Dark suit and black Homburg is best. And display almost no hand-luggage. All this will distinguish you from Nevil the Novice, who gets out of the plane in boots covered with nails, his arms full of duty free cigarettes and his Customs declaration held between his teeth. This is bad travel play. Allow yourself to have one book as total luggage. It could be a novel by Updike – or to throw emphasis on the fact that Nevil is struggling with a foreign phrase book, a work by Camus, in French. On the subject of language, it is better, in the ski world, to talk English resolutely, although technical terms should be always in German, French or Italian.

'Like *Wedeln*,' I said.

'What's that?' said a great-niece.

'Useful word,' I said. 'It's a series, really, of short rhythmic parallel turns in the fall line, characterised by fluid continuity minimal upper body movement.' Actually I was reading this from a book held under the table.

This impressed Nevil. Good luck to him, we all said: but it is part of the ski-man's duty to make sure that novices realise that not everything is as easy as it seems. If the young learner finds it natural to take a little jump when he is changing direction, and shows signs of instinctive grace, make sure that you compliment him with a 'but'.

'Good, but you should not try this turn unless you understand the difference between hop-unweighting to make a cross parallel and the hop to land with a heel thrust.'

Slightly older beginners can be told that coming down is easy but the great question is are you sure of being able to get to the top. It all depends on the type of ski-lift. The inexorable motion of the endless cable – that's what he's got to beware of. If he's going to be towed up hanging on to a T-bar, tell him that the speed of it is adjusted so that there's *just* time for each pair of skiers to step into place, move sticks to disengaged hand, straighten skis and see that they are parallel with your partner's before you find yourself yanked forward. A chair lift, you are bound to tell them, is more difficult. It may be days before they learn to pile everything into their lap and succeed in not missing the chair altogether as it sweeps forward to deliver the dreaded undercut.

Now would be the time to mention the dangers of cold. The ski-lift is just where the coldest winds catch you. There was the case last year of the man who froze to the seat. Does your anorak have double polyester fillings? The danger of frostbite is ever present. Watch your companion's face carefully. If her nose goes white, fling her to the ground and rub her face in the snow.

'Tell me,' I said trying to draw them out. 'What is the one-up place to go to now?'

Switzerland in general, they seemed to say. Vague about the exact spot. The British need a Delightful Little Place (how to keep things cheap for the British). 'Of course,' said Jimmy, 'there's always unexplored country. "Do you realise that you have seventy-five miles of perfect *piste* here."' This was at Madonna di Campiglio. They may take you for Real Estate. Or you can say you prefer the Petit Diable to the Grand Diable because it has more *moguls* and fewer *shüsses*.

'But there will always be someone who will say "Yes, but you don't know the country in *redelschpitz* weather."'

We were getting near the basic question. How, if not an expert, to suggest that you know more than you admit, and though not actually wearing a red anorak (sign of an instructor) that you are perfectly ready to instruct.

It is quite a good thing to have regrets about some famous aspect of the ski world not being what it was. Take slalom (sliding down hill between impossibly awkwardly placed sticks). I happen to be an expert in that myself, having long been able to share the perils and regret the mistakes of the reckless from the vantage point of my television set in St John's Wood. I happened to read the ski correspondent in the *Guardian* who said that the whole thing was becoming too automatic.

'It's become too easy,' I said. 'They *must* vary the placing of the gates. All one has to do at present is to swivel the hips. Sort of rumba.'

If you are going to talk like that it is better to stick, yourself, to easy slopes, where one can look reasonable, than to a moderate slope where you may fall flat on your back. After all nobody's watching.

'Except when you finish,' said Chris, a friend rather than a relation. 'The thing to do is to practise a decisive finish without running in to the end of a queue. No harm in pointing out that although the instructors are technically perfect, not all instructors are good at racing. The French experts go like hell and just manage to keep upright. Wherever you go you want to be hairy – give the impression of breakneck speed, I mean.'

Jimmy and Chris have combined a lot of these gambits in a vivid new kind of happening. They are part of the British ski-bob team. I asked them what sort of speed they were aiming at this year.

'We ought to do a hundred to be any good,' they said. This stopped my reminiscence of being pulled along behind a trotting horse at Pontresina in the year when The Charleston was invented. When they arrived last year there were just the four of them and the Austrian team seemed to number at least ten, which included a manager and a masseur and a doctor and a wax expert. Britain was deficient in wax. 'We thought we'd put on blue,' they said, addressing the Austrian wax man personally.

'No – it is wrong, wrong. You must have part of blue to two parts of silver today – with a half of paraffin to two thirds of red ...' I am not sure of the dialogue but what pleases me is that skimanship overcomes all barriers of race and nationality. The team did well by practising a spectacular finish, twenty yards through the air, over a specially constructed bump by the Teleferique. Sometimes it coincided with the arrival of a bus load of finishing school girls.

'And what about falling?'

Good question, and what about injury?

'Personally,' said Jimmy, 'I don't think it's frightfully smooth to have a broken leg. Though some people think it's all right to be seen with a deep tan in London on crutches in January.'

'If you do fall,' said Chris, 'you don't want to make too much of a meal of it. You don't want to be taken down the hill in the blood waggon.'

Chris described this as a kind of aluminium egg poacher shaped like an ambulance.

'When I used to fall,' I said, 'I used to say I was "trying a fall." You see there's a special art –'

'Quite so,' said Jimmy, 'but it's best if you can suggest there's something wrong with your gear. Ideally you finish the run on one ski only and examine the other one in an absorbed way. It all depends who's watching, if anyone.'

Sam the Smooth, I remember, had a marvellous line with accidents. He was one of the most minor ski specialists in England. But he could slide forward on an even slope and remain upright, usually standing somewhere half way up the hill. If ever there was an accident, or even just a fall, he would slide slowly up. Especially if it was a girl, there he was, at her side.

'Don't move her,' Sam would say. 'This is my job.' Calmly, quietly he would undo the little wallet which he wore, just like an instructor, on his belt. He would tie the only bandage he knew how to tie – for a sprained ankle. The snag was that his ski-ing was so shaky that I have seen him fall just through the act of stopping by the prone object. He fell flat on his face, and it made his nose bleed.

'Snow, damn you – SNOW!'

'Probably the smoothest man in the night-club,' said Jimmy.

'Exactly,' I said. 'A great man for the après-ski.'

'That would have been when he wore his racing pants, with a stripe,' said Chris. 'Goes up with his gear to the ski-lift, sits in the sun, and takes the lift down in the afternoon.'

'Exactly,' I said. I had done this once or twice myself, but only as an experiment.

'I don't think Sam often got up much before half past eleven,' said a mother, who had not yet spoken. 'He then went down to meet the train and take a look at the beauty chorus, as they arrived.'

'How horribly true,' I said.

'Well, I used to think one wouldn't mind being the sort of woman a man wanted to come back to.'

'Of course not,' I said, instantly changing sides.

19.2.1969

The Demon Alps
(Our Artist's Dream, after reading the numerous Accidents to Mountain-Climbers.)

'Always forget from one year to another whether I need ski-sticks.'

'There's never a shortage of rich widows fighting
for these chaps' attentions.'

Michael Bywater

SKI-ING OUTFITS

Plus-fours were 'not recommended for ski-ing' when they first became fashionable, but that didn't deter Eustace, who, like all his splendid family, was in some respects barking mad. Eustace never slept indoors, ever, and had no fear of the cold. Long before It was fashionable, he was a well-known figure in Val d'Isère or Klosters, as he snow-ploughed down the mountainside, eyes tight shut, a stately figure in his deerstalker, tweed coat, plus-fours and Argyll wool stockings, dressed precisely as he would be for a day's wildfowling with the exception of a pair of antique hickory skis so long that nowadays EEC regulations would compel them to be articulated and to carry a spare driver.

Eustace is dead now, and in Arthur's bosom if ever man went to Arthur's bosom; and no bad thing, because I don't think he'd have liked it now.

The first thing you have to do nowadays is to spend a lot of money in a ski-shop. You can spend hundreds of pounds on clothing that they *say* will make you look like a suave, jet-set, cosmopolitan, a sort of waterproof James Bond. It won't. What you will look like is a ghastly swivel-eyed *arriviste* shite-hawk dressed as a DayGlo robot, but since conformity is the name of the game and everyone else will look just as repulsive, you've got what, presumably, you wanted.

The little snobberies and point-scorers within the business are fantastically complex and staggeringly silly. Everything changes from year to year. Last year, for example, I'm told that the great thing was to have a one-piece dungaree ski-suit with a sort of sandpaper bum so that if you fell over while breaking the world speed record on the black *piste* you didn't slide all the way down the mountainside to make an unexpected supine entry, into the midst of the après-ski; social death, that, especially if you're not wearing those Moon Boots with fur on the outside (why? any berk could tell you that the sensible place for the fur is on the *inside*).

This year, I imagine, the sandpaper bum will be too, too passé, my dear, partly because of the passage of time, which is the enemy of *chic*, partly because someone will have realised that to wear sandpaper on one's bum suggests that one *expects* to fall over.

And it's the same with the business end, as well, the skis and the surgical boots and the orthopaedic-looking bindings which hold the two together. Skis, I learn, are getting shorter all the time, and will soon be like flat skates; and never mind if you can get down the mountain quite happily on your old ones, you have to have the new type – a cunning move by the frauds and pace-setters which means that the poor punter, on his upward social and *sportif* spiral, gets less and less for more and more.

Same with the bindings: anything other than step-in models, which means that you can reel out of the bar and step into your skis without trouble, will just not do. (Mind you, step-in bindings have eliminated one distinction between the various grades of expertise; formerly, the better skier broke his leg on the *piste*, and the duffer broke his fingers in his bindings trying to get his skis on.) I predict that soon bindings will go out altogether, since they too suggest that you expect to fall over, and the real slickers will simply bolt their skis immovably to their boots and plunge down the slopes; there'll still be room for status-juggling, however, with old nails at the bottom of the scale and Olympic hi-tech rhodium expansion bolts at the top.

My inclination is to blame the *Sunday Times* for all this. It must be frightful for poor Harold Evans to wake up at night with the realisation that, despite the great journalistic triumphs over which he has presided, *We Learnt to Ski* is what he will be remembered for. This is the time of year when people will be digging out their much-thumbed copies and salivating over the pictures of stem turn and *Langlauf* and *téléphérique* and a large *Kümmel mit Eis bitte* and applying, against all hope, for gold American Express cards; this, too, is the season when every other damned telephone call is some half-witted 'acquaintance' who's just ringing to say he's arranging a small party to Val d'Isère, just twelve of us, it'll be a laugh, only £1,800 for the ten days and can you let me know by Thursday because I've got to send the deposit off?

What can one say? Where do they get the money from? Why do they want to spend it on *that*? You can't just say sod off, I can't afford it, I don't like it, I'm a married man, I'm a Roman Catholic, I've a weak ankle, short sight, the wrong-shaped head for a woolly hat, a Siamese cat and a harpsichord to look after, I HATE THE WHOLE IDEA.

It wouldn't be fair. It's kind of them to ask. And you can pack a lot in for your £1,800, plus £250 for the skis, £200 for the boots, £185 for the bindings, £350 all in for the clothing (not including après-ski gear); for that outlay you can get frostbite, break your leg, poison your liver, get snow-blindness and herpes, go bankrupt, be snubbed by people, snub other people, get the other sort of herpes, cracked lips, smashed teeth and sunburn (of the face only, so that, nude, you look like a slug in a balaclava) and go home to divorce proceedings and a month in hospital.

Terribly sorry; I'll be busy that fortnight. Call me antisocial, Thoreauist, pariah, my idea of ski-ing remains somewhere I can ski in my incompetent manner, crouched on ancient skis like an invalid, and nobody sneers or thinks I should do better; where I

can wear my corduroy trousers and my old jersey and my lambskin shapeless hat and nobody tries to persuade me into luminous nylon; where there still are beat-up mountain men hauling logs on horse sleds to remind you that you're not in a playground provided by God for the improvement of one's *amour-propre*; and where the ski-shop is in the basement of a house, run by a farmer who does it part-time, and who will provide skis but assumes that you've brought your own clothes.

It will never become fashionable, because it won't – or can't – pander to consumerism; the day we found a kilo of sausage in a village shop after a three-mile walk through the snow, we celebrated wildly.

The place does exist, surprisingly. It also has a few disadvantages; for example, shortly after, but unconnected with (I hope) my last holiday there, it was invaded. Sorry. It invaded itself, and Moscow had nothing to do with it. The place is Poland, in the Tatra mountains; it is, for the moment, rather hard for me to go there; but the tweedy, *Schüss*ing ghost of Eustace, unconstrained by such silliness as martial law and closed borders, is probably enjoying it enormously. It's his sort of place.

29.9.1982

R. G. G. Price

YOUR HOLIDAY HEALTH

One of those Medical Columns

The risks of a foreign holiday can be slightly reduced with forethought. Your health-bag should include not merely ordinary first aid equipment – bandages, artery-forceps, emetics – but a wide range of drugs capable of fighting many of the local diseases. Foreign physicians should be consulted only in extreme emergencies. Women should always be accompanied by two powerful friends when visiting one of them. A handkerchief soaked in a strong disinfectant should be held to the nose in the waiting-room. Never pay the fee demanded without haggling.

Sunlight abroad can be as deadly as a tarantula. Expose yourself to it for only five minutes the first day, increasing by an equal amount every twenty-four hours. Never sunbathe within two hours of a meal. It is more than unwise to let foreigners see bare skin apart from face and hands. There is little self-control across the Channel.

Foreign food is a danger that can be avoided by taking all food with you. Shop around for a portable larder. Never, on any account, even threats from chefs, touch shellfish, made-up dishes, cold meat – how long has it been cold? – or milk. Insist on seeing all water boiled at your table. Take your temperature one and a quarter hours after every meal. If you simply must use a restaurant, take a seat near the door and hold a tube of anti-burns jelly: foreign stoves often explode and fire-precautions are rudimentary. Do not get drawn into conversations by other diners. You will not know whether they are making remarks to which you should take exception. Also, if you have broken the ice, it may be difficult to deal with them firmly enough should a panic rush occur. Your only real hope of digesting a meal without danger of ulcers is equanimity.

Never leave your bedroom without being prepared for rabies, tetanus, wolves or sharks, and berserk inhabitants. You should take a mild sedative throughout the vacation and heavily increase the dose if upset by electric eels, purse-snatchers, vendettas or the police. Unlike our fatherly British bobbies, they are not on your side. If interrogated in the basement of a police station, get a friend to photograph your injuries when you emerge. You will probably prefer it to be a friend of the same sex.

Visiting sights can cause painful swellings of the ankles. Theatres and the like involve association with large numbers of people who do not share our standards of health and hygiene. Casinos can cause apoplexy and stress-acne. It will give you a better chance of reaching home again if you confine your pleasures to cards or gossip with fellow members of your party. In many countries, the inhabitants cheat or become violent if they lose. What began as a simple game of tennis or pelota can end in bloodshed. In some places, of the kind that travel agents praise for remoteness, the duel is not dead. Make certain before you leave that at least one of your party can give a blood transfusion. You should have your blood-group tattooed prominently.

With a sensible regimen, a good supply of drugs and the minimum contact with place and people, the inevitable risks can generally be kept within bounds and it should be possible, in many cases, to return home little the worse.

26.1.1977

'I'm always glad when the tourist season's over.'

ffolkes's

GRAND VICTORIAN PACKAGE TOUR

'Something tells me that isn't going to help either.'

*'I had hoped that we would have kept off the
question of whether or not they should join the
Industrial Revolution.'*

'I'm afraid this is as far as we go. You'll have to walk to Dover.'

'I think this is where our little group might split up for
an hour or so. I'm sure the ladies would like to see the
Cathédrale.'

'Madre de Dios! It's Plague, War, Famine, Death, and the
British Holidaymaker!'

'Another thing about
Liechtenstein – their
road maps are
really easy to fold.'

Guy Bellamy

A NEW MAN

A short story

The battered old Comet 4, sold off cheaply to Broomstick Airlines by a nationalised outfit who had replaced it with something safer, rose in the morning sun and missed the Pyrenees by a few vital inches. At his window seat, Roy Smith dropped the paperback he was reading into a hold-all between his feet and peered out of the window at the area where green Spain meets dry Spain. Among the cheap package holidaymakers who were gabbling now in a multiplicity of British accents he felt at home: nothing much had ever happened to him, either.

By some kind of oversight he had never even been abroad, holidaying damply in Cornwall or Wales with his plastic mac when others flew off, after the obligatory delays, with their Ambre Solaire. He wouldn't be here now – listening morbidly for any significant changes in the tone of the Comet's engines – if he had not won the holiday in a competition. At first he had tried to sell it and then to give it away but the people where he worked at the Ministry of Agriculture had become exasperated by the acute lethargy which they diagnosed in him and were determined that, at the age of thirty, he should be turfed from his enervating rut, if only for a couple of weeks. He told them that he couldn't go away now, he was waiting to hear about some promotion, but they promised to send him a telegram if any news came through. Get on the plane, they said. Fly to the sun. You'll be a new man.

The plane dipped over Barcelona and headed hopefully out to sea. Far below he could see dozens of tiny boats ploughing across the Mediterranean, but he had no means of knowing their real size. Soon afterwards the Comet began to lose height, and then the old stone farmhouses and ancient Arab waterwheels of Majorca came to greet them. Roy had read a lot about the island. Georges Sand and Chopin and Robert Graves had lived here. The mountains were higher than Ben Nevis. He stared out of the window at Palma's crowded airport.

Half an hour later the holiday trade's erratic efficiency had deposited Roy with thirty other holidaymakers on a coach headed south. They arrived very quickly at a sky-scraper hotel in the woods at Las Maravillas. Roy and five others were dropped off, and the coach rolled slowly on in search of more identical hotels. In his third-floor room he unpacked and washed, and then went out to his balcony to look over the trees at Palma Bay, less than a hundred yards away. The temperature was in the high seventies and the sky was a deep blue from one horizon to another. It wasn't like Cornwall at all.

He decided to go down to the bar to see who he would be spending this fortnight with. He had never adjusted easily to leisure: like many insecure men he worked more hours than he had to.

The bar opened on to a patio strewn with tables, and beyond was the hotel's swimming pool where most of the guests, appreciably browner than today's arrivals, were now entertaining themselves. But at the bar itself were all five of the people who had arrived on Roy's coach and he placed himself near them when he ordered a beer in the hope that productive conversation would break out.

There was a middle-aged lady who looked like a new widow spending the insurance, and an obviously married couple – obviously, because they weren't bothering to talk to each other. The man was about forty, short, ill at ease in a new, bright holiday shirt, and his wife, an attractive woman in her thirties, gazed into the distance looking strangely lonely despite the constant company of her spouse. Next to the widow was a young man of about Roy's age who looked like Covent Garden out of Nine Elms and could hardly have been anything but a used-car salesman. He was wearing a check suit with waistcoat and flamboyant tie, and had a vicious pencil-line moustache.

'Fit me up, squire,' he said, pushing his empty glass towards the young Spanish barman. Near them all but evidently unattached to any of them was a blonde girl of about twenty who had been the sixth arrival on the coach. As she walked down the bar to fetch herself a stool Roy found himself gazing at a bottom that would have disturbed a eunuch. She returned to order a chocolate drink called a Lumumba – he might have been murdered, Roy thought, but at least he had a drink named after him.

'Danny,' said the used-car salesman in answer to a question from the widowed lady.

'Mrs Stapleton,' she said. 'Is your wife with you?'

'Wife?' said Danny. 'Do me a favour. As it happens, I was married once.'

'It broke down?' suggested Mrs Stapleton.

'It broke down and then it broke up. There's nothing better on earth than a woman for a couple of hours – but twenty-five years? Leave me out!' He pushed his glass at the barman again. 'Fit me up. Muchas gracias.'

'I expect that you'll find a partner here,' said Mrs Stapleton. 'They call it the Isle of Love. What about those two girls over there with their mother?'

She nodded towards a table where a woman sat with two pale overweight girls who yawned a lot.

'On a scale of one to five I'd give them one,' said Danny. 'But who's the bird who arrived on the coach with us? Different class, that.'

'Melanie,' said Mrs Stapleton. 'She's on my floor. I'll introduce you.'

'You can borrow my wife if you like,' said the married man who had been listening to this in silence. 'No visible scars. Never raced or rallied.'

His wife smiled apologetically at his outrageous wit, but Mrs Stapleton ignored them and beckoned Melanie from her stool.

'This is Danny,' she said and Melanie smiled warily. She had shoulder-length hair and blue eyes that looked as if life had hurt her at some time.

'Have a drink, Melanie,' said Danny. 'And you, Mrs Stapleton. Am I buying a round? Hold me back, someone.'

As the laughter rose and fell around Danny, Roy studied Melanie. All women were attractive for the first hour: the flaws emerged slowly. But he smiled to himself even as he thought it. How did he know that the flaws emerged slowly? There *had* been a girl once whom he had mislaid through some carelessness but all he could recall now from his most potent years was launching himself on a couple of hundred unsuccessful Saturday night searches for a short-sighted, well-scrubbed nymphomaniac with big breasts. A civil servant called Roy Smith was not the magic combination that brought even lonely girls running, and he was now a very objective observer of women.

The married man, having failed to break into the main conversation, touched him on the shoulder.

'First time here?' he asked.

Roy nodded. 'You?'

'We come every year. My name's Butler, by the way. This is my wife.'

'Roy,' said Roy.

'We like it,' said Mrs Butler. 'It used to be so cheap. Forty pounds for two weeks and that wasn't so long ago.'

'It's still cheap,' said Mr Butler.

'Yes, but not so cheap,' said his wife.

Mrs Stapleton swung round on her stool, clearly anxious to retain her role of mistress of ceremonies.

'Introduce us to your new friend,' she told Mr Butler.

'This is Troy,' he announced.

'That's a nice name,' said Melanie.

So it is, thought Roy. He tried to think of a suitably Troy-like salutation.

'Hi,' he said.

'What do you do, Troy?' asked Danny. 'I'm a car dealer myself.'

Roy decided that a Troy wouldn't blab that easily. He snapped his fingers and winked. 'Sometimes I sits and drinks and sometimes I just drinks,' he said.

Everybody laughed. Melanie moved her stool a little so that Roy was brought well into the range of her vision.

'Man of mystery,' she murmured. Roy winked. He wondered whether to snap his fingers as well, but he didn't want to overdo it. A juke-box in the corner of the bar had just completed an old Shadows record, *The Rise And Fall Of Flingel Bunt,* and now moved on to Helen Shapiro.

'Am I correct in thinking,' asked Mrs Stapleton, 'that the records on this juke-box are curiously dated?'

'I make you right,' said Danny. 'Helen Shapiro already! You remember this one, Troy? You look old enough.'

A Roy would have nodded sadly at the lost years that had slipped unused through his fingers – but a Troy? Something quick, something witty, something mildly ribald. 'Sure do Danny boy,' he said. 'Those were the days when a left breast lasted you two and a half hours.'

Everybody laughed loudly at his little joke – they had been born too soon as well – but Roy's mind was already racing ahead. It was going to be a busy afternoon.

Six hours later he stood in front of his bathroom mirror and considered the results. The pale and slightly unhealthy-looking young man who was wasting the best years of his life studying fatstock subsidies in the Appropriation Accounts and Data Processing Division had disappeared. Only a cretin would mistake the fine figure in the mirror for a humble civil servant (clerical grade).

His hair, which had been long and of a somewhat greasy disposition, had been shampooed, cut dramatically and styled. Two hours on the beach had given him the beginnings of a promising tan. A black silk shirt had replaced the nondescript Marks and Spencer product that he had worn that morning; a pair of tight, white trousers hugged his hips and his old sandals had given way to a pair of Kickers. As a final touch, a gold chain hung round his newly-bronzed neck and a matching but chunkier version was clamped round his right wrist. Hi Troy, he said.

He took the lift to reception, which was crowded with sullen-faced Germans, and left the hotel. Along the seafront the restaurants, bars and nightclubs were filling up with determined pleasure-seekers as the sun sank finally over the bay. Troy bought himself some Capote cigars and studied the night-spots: he was going to be the man who knew where the action was. He sauntered back to the hotel eventually, polishing his aphorisms. The others were at their usual place at the bar.

'Troy!' said Melanie. 'Where have you been all day?'

'You know how it is,' said Troy, grabbing a stool and placing it very close to her. 'As Buckminster Fuller used to say, men are born with feet and not roots, and I'm into mobility.' He had great difficulty in not being distracted by a vividly detailed mental picture of how that would have gone down in the Appropriation Accounts and Data Processing Division.

'I've missed you,' said Melanie, pouting.

'Separation is amputation,' agreed Troy, puffing on his cigar. 'Gin?'

'Let me get them,' said Mrs Stapleton, studying, as discreetly as was possible, Troy's new appearance. 'I always know when I've drunk too much – I start buying people drinks.'

'Nice gear, Troy,' said Danny. 'You're a new man.'

Melanie lent forward on her stool and put her mouth against Troy's ear. 'He wants to sleep with me,' she whispered.

'A gentleman of taste and discernment,' Troy whispered back.

Encouraged, she took his hand. 'Blow in my ear and I'll follow you anywhere.' He looked into her pale blue eyes and saw longing, devotion, capitulation. Jesus Christ, he thought uneasily. He got a Troylike grip on himself.

'I know a good night club round the corner,' he suggested.

Mrs Stapleton handed him his drink. 'My room number is 402, Troy,' she said. 'In case you get lonely.'

'I'll remember it.'

'And mine's 465,' said Mrs Butler, clutching a bottle of cheap champagne. 'I'll kick the old man out.'

Mr Butler rocked drunkenly on the next stool. 'Never raced or rallied,' he muttered.

Danny leant on the bar and stared at the new twosome. Troy, watching, recognised the twitch of envy that had hitherto been a part of his own personality disorders. He swallowed his drink and stood up, holding Melanie's hand. 'We're night-clubbing,' he told them. 'Hasta mañana.'

'Some people have got it, and some people haven't got it,' said Mrs Stapleton. 'But that young man is just loaded down with it.'

'Don't worry about him,' said Danny, offering the barman his empty glass. 'Danny is available. Fit me up, squire.' He bent forward and spoke drunkenly into Mrs Stapleton's ear, but she was a battle-scarred veteran of many a sexual frolic and, if she no longer knew how to attract, she was still justly proud of her deflection technique.

'What did he say?' asked Mrs Butler.

'What did you say turns you on?' asked Mrs Stapleton.

'Pubic hair,' said Danny. 'As it happens.'

Mrs Stapleton put a sympathetic hand on

his shoulder. 'I'll bring you some down in the morning, dear.'

Troy woke abruptly at four o'clock and wondered what had disturbed him. Beside him lay Melanie, her hungry mouth finally closed, but she was deeply asleep and could not have been the cause of his waking. Then he heard someone with long finger-nails tapping gently at his bedroom door.

'Troy,' a voice whispered. 'It's Mrs Stapleton.'

He lay very still and after a few more taps and calls he heard her slippers flopping despondently down the stone corridor. Exhausted by the night's activity, he went back to sleep quickly but there was a faint smile on his face which Melanie vainly misunderstood when she woke him at ten.

Later that morning he left her to rinse some clothes, and was ambushed by Mrs Butler on the seafront. She was fresh from the hotel's hairdresser and was refulgent in a dazzling summer dress that took three or four years off her age.

'There you are, Troy,' she said, as if this was the triumphant conclusion to a long and challenging search. 'Good time, in the night-club?'

'Hi,' said Troy. 'Yeah, tremendous.'

Mrs Butler looked up at him: her face registered concern. 'Isn't she a little young for you?'

'Young?'

'Melanie. What is she – nineteen? Twenty?'

'Twenty-two.'

'You should read *In Praise Of Older Women*, Troy.'

'Room 465,' said Troy with a wink.

'You remembered!' said Mrs Butler, and then added cryptically: 'Bill's got a bad back.'

He escaped before further presumably harrowing details of her husband's incapacities could be imposed on him – Mrs Butler's unequivocal approach suggested that she would settle for nothing less than a midnight assignation, if not a divorce.

But within a few crowded days it became accepted that Troy belonged to Melanie. He entertained her with style, keeping both them and his bank cheque card busy. They toured Roman and Moorish remains. They took a boat round the bay. They visited the walled city of Alcudia, the glass-blowers of Manacor, the elephants in the African reserve. They went across the island to Porto Cristo and the Caves of Drach to see Europe's largest underground lake; and they still found time to lie for hours on the beach.

'The trees in the orange groves are a thousand years old but they still bear fruit,'

Melanie told them all in the bar; the others never seemed to travel more than a mile from the hotel.

'You two young ones certainly get about,' said Mrs Stapleton. 'Personally I thought it a little too windy today.'

'It was,' Melanie agreed. 'I wore this dress and the wind went right through me.'

'Lucky old wind,' Danny grunted. No longer the cynosure of the group, he had perceptibly less panache than the man who had arrived bubbling on this island a week ago.

'I think Benny is a fan of yours,' said Mr Butler.

'Danny, not Benny.'

'Can you hold it for another five minutes? My wife lost her ring around here when we were on a boating holiday last year.'

'Sorry. I'm hopeless at names. What are you two up to tomorrow?'

'The bullfight,' said Troy. 'It should be fun if the wind stays up. It's the matador's enemy. Plays havoc with his cape. Matador's enemy, matelot's friend.'

His audience listened willingly, hungry for more. Troy knew things.

'I dunno where you find the energy,' said Danny. 'I get shattered sitting in a deckchair.' Troy bought them all drinks, and Danny gazed at his thoughtfully. 'If I'm fed up I like to get drunk, and if I'm happy I like to get drunk. Funny that.'

'I'll give you some room numbers to cheer you up,' said Troy. 'I've got a few to spare.'

It was late in the second week of his holiday that Melanie came into the dining room as Troy was eating what the hotel wittily referred to as breakfast. Today they were going to hire a Seat and drive up through Inca to the mountains in the north of the island to find the bit that was higher than Ben Nevis.

Melanie handed him an envelope.

'It's a telegram for you, but look at this. It's addressed to Roy Smith. Roy. Not Troy. Isn't that a laugh?'

Troy looked at the name on the envelope and saw that she was right. He opened it and pulled out a telegram that read: SORRY ROY. CAROLE GILKS GOT THE PROMOTION. He stared at it for some time and then folded it up.

'Bad news?' asked Melanie.

He shook his head.

'Well, come on then. We've got to get moving. We have a mountain to visit.'

He pushed the news from the Appropriation Accounts and Data Processing Division into his back trouser pocket and shook his head again, very slowly. Melanie looked at him curiously.

'Drive all up there just to look at a mountain?' said Roy. 'I don't think so. No, I don't think so. No, I don't think so.'

11.4.1979

'Typical! Some bastard's nicked the disabled mooring.'

'Personally I don't mind heavy weather. I rather like roughing it.'
'Roughing it is the very word, Sir, with your natty little muffler an' only six meals a day.'

Libby Purves

CHANNEL FEVER

One o'clock in the morning, a fine fish dinner settling uneasily under the final cognac, one hand outstretched to dowse the oil lamp, and the last thing you want is a juddering thump up the stern and a shrill cry of 'MERDE' out of the moonless dark.

Spend the night in a small French harbour, though, and that is what you are likely to get. It is what we got in Port Tudy, Ile de Groix, off the coast of Britanny. Hunching out of the cabin onto the deck of our 26 ft stretch of British Territory, we prepared to sell our lives dearly. Alongside us, from the raft of little yachts moored hugger-mugger from one side of Port Tudy to the other, the natives crept out to investigate the sound of battering and mayhem. A larger yacht, it seemed, had tied up cavalierly to the tunnyboat's bit of wall. The tunnyboat had returned.

The subsequent colourful five minutes, and a fresh north-easterly wind, had brought the yacht, its anchor-chain inexplicably wound around its propeller, to rest uneasily against the stern of *le petit bateau anglais*. We, its masters, now stood displaying stiff upper lips, striped Harrods pyjamas, and a pre-war timber boat-hook sportingly turned blunt side on to the lunging, battering bows. From the boats alongside, figures popped up in André Jamet sleepwear crying *Hop La!* and *Voyons!* and expanding chic telescopic boat-hooks with flicks of their wrists.

'What is passing itself?' we all cried. A new yacht loomed mysteriously out of the darkness, a figure on the bow noisily revealing that it was not his own anchor cable that the *sacré* pig had wound around his propeller, but that of the speaker. Doggedly, the crews of the tossing boats held off the drifters, broadside on, with outstretched boat-hooks.

Thirty-five minutes later, the scene was unchanged except that most of us had reversed our boat-hooks to gouge sharp-end-first into the attackers, and the wind had risen by several pounds' pressure on the biceps. The French yachts either side of us had begun to make a night of it, laughing uproariously and offering jocular advice to the helpless, tangled intruders. Aboard *le petit bateau anglais,* mugs of tea were sipped through ever tighter lips, and a heartfelt mutter arose: 'If this were England,' it went, 'a Leader would have emerged by now to sort this nonsense out.'

He was quite right. Someone – be he retired naval officer or tough young clever-dick, efficient or merely bossy, would have evolved in any English harbour in such disorder, and outlined a Plan for us all to follow sheepishly, heaving and towing until everyone was tied up soundly and tucked back in his bunk. The next morning, rowing sedately to the lavatories or shaking out the sleeping bags, we would all have agreed that it was a terrible business, could have been nasty, fortunate Not More Damage Caused. And one particularly thoughtful and literate skipper would have penned a censorious article for *Yachting Monthly* about the Very Real Dangers of inadequate mooring lines, or poorly signposted fishing berths, or rum te tiddley ido. We take things damn seriously, we British yachtsmen.

The French, on the other hand, were all *en vacances*; the incident another pleasurable adventure, the terror of damage lessened by compulsory insurance and (muttered the more defiantly striped pyjamas present) natural irresponsibility. The next morning at Port Tudy, nobody even thought the fracas worth mentioning, much, except for a few tasteless jokes about our boat-hook. We sailed with dignity to look for emptier harbours.

Indeed, if you want to experience a real clash of national temperaments, a real sense of the Foreign, you could not do better than to take up sailing small boats from one side of the Channel to the other. Forget all that stuff about The China Experience, or The Soul of Middle America; nowhere is quite so foreign as France, provided you have sailed to it.

There are two reasons for this, as far as I can see: first, the indisputable fact that a country you have won by staying up most of the night struggling with flapping wet sails, getting rained on for hours and terrified out of your wits in the fog; a country you have had to *find* by drawing lines on a damp chart while you feel sick, and waving an unpleasant little crackling Morse machine at the horizon, feels ineffably alien and exotic from the start. The first time I sailed from South-ampton to Deauville, I felt like Marco Polo.

The second reason is less edifying: whereas a land tourist is under the foreign-ers' roof, a guest with society manners, on your own boat you are in Britain. You fly a huge red ensign from your main staff and only a miserable little nylon *tricolore* at the cross-trees for courtesy. You are at home. You can make proper tea, and eat rice pudding, and listen to *The Archers,* and not alter one single value.

I once cringed below decks at Deauville, listening to a particularly patrician crew of Hooray Henries hailing the dignified, cultured, anglophile harbourmaster: 'Alors, mon froggy old person, où peut-on get a good hot tub et un pint de Badger Bitter, then?' It must be something of the same spirit which makes Frenchmen, arriving in British marinas full of nice families feeding sandwiches to their children, invariably leap straight to the rail and pee triumphantly into the water.

All this lurking hostility is exacerbated by the fact that if you give an Englishman a yacht, he immediately becomes more British

than ever before, clips his speech drastically, and performs every small manoeuvre with a seriousness worthy of docking *Britannia* in the Pool of London. The English crew approaching a wall or anchorage takes fanati-cal pride in its almost total silence; every man, woman and child clutches the appro-priate rope or fender with fierce concen-tration, and no word is spoken except 'Haa-aar – OKAY' and perhaps 'Ve'y good'.

They then look on in horror while a French boat steams in four times as fast, shattering the peace of the evening with hys-terical cries of 'Non, non, NON, Jean-Claude, par ici, AH MON DIEU, ça va aller, AHIEEEEE no NON par ici, quoi,' and then tying up just as well as the Brits did, more or less. The pleasure *we* get from yachting is a profound and serious one, with a lurking suggestion of administering a national sac-rament; we are, in short, deeply pompous. The Frog, clearly one of nature's cads, regards it as just another branch of Le Sport.

He educates himself, too, as parvenus will. We learn by example and error and LEA navigation classes; he admits without shame that he went to an *Ecole de Voile*, and sets up thousands more. Show him a crack in the rocks on the most inhospitable jag of the Biscay coast, and he will shove a concrete ramp up it and lead out an inexhaustible stream of aggressive infants in cockleshell dinghies, training hard as part of his scheme to nick the Admiral's Cup off us in 1994.

Look around Millbay Dock in Plymouth the night before a Transatlantic race: you will see French yachtsmen twanging fiercely at their rigging, while the British assemble aboard the boat with most whisky, dashing back only to haul their flags down at 2100 hrs precisely.

So I suppose 1982 will be another summer of confrontation in the fearful cultural bou-illabaisse of the Channel marinas: cheery boatloads of Frenchmen with red setters will bump past Jack Hawkins fantasists in white-topped caps, chipping off their navy paintwork with gay cries of 'Oh pardon, c'est pas grave'; figure-hugging, pastel-striped Breton knitwear will dry provocatively alongside huge snaggled blue sweaters; strangled county shrieks will greet calloused foreign palms as they slap merrily on Lilly-whites' best beach shorts. Noble, grizzled heirs of Bligh and Nelson will choke on their pipes at Benodet as girls in G-strings swing their unfettered bosoms recklessly over moving winches, hoisting vulgar striped sails to the warm wind.

I am copping out, myself. We shall sail to Ireland. Or Iceland. Or Norway. France is altogether too far away.

20.1.1982

'We're on a pretty tight schedule, so we won't have time to take in the whole thing.
Can you just give us a brief outline?'

DRAWING-ROOM INANITIES.

He. '*I wonder you're not afraid of going to Nice after those
terrible earthquakes!*'
She. '*Oh, surely those things are always confined to the poorer
quarters of the town!*'

Mahood

HOLIDAY EXCHANGE

English family wish to exchange house in Surrey for apartment in New York. Apply to Rodney Smithers, Box 179354

'Can you do a Brooklyn accent? They want us to chat to their plants!'

'Hello, Mrs Birnbaum? It's Emma Smithers—oh sorry I forgot about the time difference but there's someone here who wants your opinion on urban blight, bussing, the Presidential hopefuls, financing New York ...'

'... Apparently Hiram Birnbaum is her second husband and Lucille is his third wife and she is having an affair with her hairdresser on the advice of her shrink and they are trying to get custody of the dogs from their last marriages—this beats a re-run of "Upstairs, Downstairs" anytime!'

*'My God, it **is** a matriarchal society!'*

'I paused for a moment in the subway!'

Mahood

HOLIDAY EXCHANGE

American family wish to swap apartment in New York for house in Surrey. Write to Hiram Birnbaum, Box 193721

'*I can't do anything about them, Honey—you know what animal lovers the English are!*'

'*Those must be the family heirlooms we are to be so careful of.*'

'*...Buckingham Palace. January 6: Today being the Feast of Epiphany, Holy Communion was celebrated in the Chapel Royal, St. James's Palace, when the customary offerings of Gold, Frankincense and Myrrh were made on behalf of the Queen by Lieutenant-Commander John Holdsworth, RN, and Lieutenant-Colonel Sir Julian Paget, Bt (Gentlemen Ushers to Her Majesty) ...*'

'*Now I can understand how that guy Clive Barnes became such a sourpuss!*'

'*I warned you that draughts are not the same thing as air conditioning!*'

Frank Muir

THE CORSICAN CONNECTION

The first time I saw Corsica it looked like a piece of coke which had been dropped into a puddle. But that was twenty-five years ago and I was looking down 20,000 feet from the cabin of a Super Constellation – that bent banana of an aircraft – which was vibrating its way towards Rome.

The next time I saw Corsica, 'The Scented Isle', was some fifteen years ago when I was taken unexpectedly rich and spent the lot taking my family for a month's holiday at Ile-Rousse. Corsica looked nothing at all like a piece of coke once we were on it. Snow-capped granite mountains surrounded Calvi airport – which in those days consisted of a wide path with a wooden hut at the end of it and had all the earmarks of a forced-landing site – and the smell of the maquis hit us in hot waves. It smelled of curry powder.

Our hotel was on a red rock in Ile-Rousse harbour. It was brand new, rated three stars, the plastic tiles were already starting to curl off the bathroom walls, the wind tore through the plastic venetian blinds at night setting up a rattle like a hundred typists taking a speed test and the month's stay cost an arm and a leg, but it was a good base to get away from and have a look around.

From the hotel we had a good view of the medieval villages of Monticello and Santa Reparata which, like most Corsican villages, clung a prudent six hundred feet or so up the mountainside to give the villagers a head start when the Corsairs and Saracen pirates arrived. One afternoon we drove up to Monticello, saw its tiny square, its elders playing boules, the little hotel and bar, packs of small children throwing rocks and half-killing each other, and that was that: we have been back to Monticello every year ever since. Monticello is now in our blood. And it is only fair to add that since we acquired a hovel there and have to do our own repairs quite a bit of our blood is in Monticello.

Although Corsica is so near, very few people know much about it and the little they do know is usually wrong. For instance, there are no bandits there – the last genuine Corsican bandit died early in the century; a benign, patriarchal figure with a gigantic white beard who spent his last few years obligingly cradling his musket and posing for picture-postcard photographers.

Nor is Napoleon the national hero – when he was a young hot-headed politician running for office the Corsicans booted him out and he had to flee to France where, you will recall, he did rather better. Corsica's hero is the extraordinary Pasquale Paoli, the eighteenth-century genius who unified the country, created a university and formulated a democratic constitution which was the envy of contemporary political theorists like Rousseau. Paoli's plans for Corsica might well have influenced the thinking of the founders of America's Constitution (Thomas Jefferson, third president of the United States, retired to a plantation which he named 'Monticello').

Although Corsica is now a *département* of France and French is the official language, nothing is more certain to infuriate a Corsican than to say that he is French. He is not. He is Corsican. Since the French acquired the island in a rather haphazard fashion from bankrupt Genoa in the early eighteenth century, they have tried to bring the island in line with other French *départements*, requiring the inhabitants to hand in their guns – about as welcome a move as asking members of the Gourmet Club to hand in their false teeth – and keeping the island utterly dependent financially on the French mainland.

But Corsicans are used to being occupied by foreign countries. Almost every Mediterranean power has tried to conquer the place; Greeks and Romans shivered with malaria on the plains near Aleria for over five hundred years, the Pope claimed the island for a while, Genoa fought Pisa for it and won and handed it over to the Bank of St George to extort all it could in the way of taxes, the Saracens were in there for a while; even the British owned it for two years, 1794–1796, after a campaign during which Nelson lost his eye on a rock above Calvi citadel whilst directing artillery fire. But claiming the island was not the same thing as subduing the inhabitants, a near-impossibility until roads were built because of the mountains, the hidden villages, and the forests and maquis into which hundreds of men could disappear in a moment.

So with that history behind them it is hardly surprising that Corsicans have little love for their latest conquerors, manage to teach their own language to their children in spite of government displeasure and refer to France not even as France but as, derisively, *le continent*.

The French, on their part, treat Corsicans as a bit of a joke, as a lot of work-shy hicks. A typical French joke tells of the Corsican walking along a pavement in Marseilles. He sees a 100 franc note in the gutter. 'Ah bon!' he says to himself. 'If I come this way tomorrow I will pick that up.'

It is true that they are sometimes not very practical. Just after Napoleon died it was decided to erect a huge statue to him in Ajaccio, his birthplace, so a mighty granite plinth was carved out of the rock in a hollow just north of Algajola. When it was finished and lay there in all its glory, a perfectly chiselled column some sixty feet long by ten feet

'No, we don't speak French, but when we're in France we speak our own language with a foreign intonation.'

in diameter, somebody must have smitten his forehead with the heel of his palm and cried the Corsican equivalent of 'Oh Gawd! How do we get it *out* of there?' Of course there was no way it could be got out. And there it lies still. About a thousand tons of it.

Nor are Corsicans very reliable on things like their own geography. Ask three old sons of the soil which mountain is Monte Cinto, the tallest, and three arms will point immediately to three different mountain tops.

The truth is that Corsicans are shepherds, not peasants. They have bulging forearms like Popeye from milking their sheep to make Rocquefort cheese and they look dour and villainous, but they are kind, funny and, like most peoples who live a simple life in hard country, they have a long tradition of hospitality to travellers and strangers. And they have the shepherd's philosophy towards making money. Ask a peasant if he would like to earn a franc and he will say, 'Yes, please!' and add it to his savings in the sock under the floorboards. Ask a shepherd if he would like to earn a franc and he is liable to reply, 'No, thank you very much. I've got one.'

The pace of life is slow in Corsica. Long conversations tend to get in the way of doing what you set out across the square to do. Except for the six weeks from the middle of August to the end of September when all France goes on holiday and most of it seems

TRICKS UPON TRAVELLERS.
Bonsor (down upon little Stannery, who's a great boaster about his 'Swell' acquaintance, and his extensive
'Travel,' and this year especially, down Palestine way). *'Did you see the Dardanelles?'*
Stannery. *'Eh? The – eh? Oh, ye' – yes! Jolly Fellars as ever I met! Dined with 'em at Viennah!'*
[Little S. has left the Club.]

to arrive in Corsica there is almost nobody about. You drive slowly on a journey, partly so as not to miss the pine forests and the waterfalls and the incredible view of the sea over a sudden precipice, but mainly so that you don't drive over the precipice. Blind corners and sudden hairpin bends over dead drops abound. I once startled the café in the square by staggering in and announcing that I had just driven the notoriously dangerous cliff road from Porto to Calvi. 'I have just done,' I announced proudly, 'five hundred bends!' The effect was electric. Men went pale. A triple Pastis was thrust into my hand and a chair was brought forward for willing hands to lower me into. Only some time later did I discover that my wobbly grasp of French had let me down and I had confused the word *virages* (bends) with the word *vierges* (virgins).

What I am really trying to say is – don't go to Corsica. If you rent one of those white concrete chalets down South and sit on the beach all day watching the waves you will only end up realising that you could do more or less the same thing on the Costa Brava or at Bournemouth for half the price. And if you take off along the coast, or inland, and get to know the Corsicans and their country then you are finished: you will never, ever want to go anywhere else.

26.1.1977

Sir Francis Burnand

CATCHING THE EARLY BOAT

In Bed: at the Highland Hotel, Oban. – What an extraordinary thing is the mechanism of the human mind! Went to sleep last night impressed with vital importance of waking at six, to catch early steamer to Gairloch. And here I am – broad awake – at exactly 5.55! Is it automatic action or what? Like setting clockwork for explosive machine. When the time comes, I blow up – I mean, *get* up. Think out this simile – rather a good one ... Need not have been so particular in telling Boots to call me, after all. Shall I get up *before* he comes? He'll be rather surprised when he knocks at the door, and hears me singing inside like a lark. But, on reflection, isn't it rather *petty* to wish to astonish an Hotel Boots? And why on earth should I get up myself, when I've tipped another fellow to get me up? But suppose he forgets to call me. I've no right, as yet, to *assume* that he will. To get up now would argue want of confidence in him – might hurt his feelings. I will give him another five minutes, poor fellow ...

Getting Up. – No actual necessity to get up yet, but, to make assurance doubly – something or other, forget what – I will ... I do. Portmanteau rather refractory; retreats under bed – quite ten minutes before I can coax it out ... When I have, it won't let me pack it. That's the worst of this breed of brown portmanteaus – they're always nasty-tempered. However, I am getting a few things into it now, by degrees. Very annoying – as fast as I put them in, this confounded portmanteau shoots them out again! If I've put in that pair of red and white striped pyjamas once, I've done it twenty times – and they always come twisting and rolling out at the back, somehow. Fortunate I left myself ample time.

Man next door to me is running it rather fine. *He* has to catch the boat, too, and he's not up yet! Hear the Boots hammering away at his door. How *can* a fellow, just for the sake of a few more minutes in bed – which he won't even know he's *had*! – go and risk losing his steamer in that way? I'll do him a good turn – knock at the wall myself. 'Hi! get up, you lazy beggar. Look sharp – you'll be late!' He thanks me, in a muffled tone, through the wall. He is a remarkably quick dresser, he tells me – it won't take him thirty-five seconds to pack, dress, pay his bill, and get on board. If that's the case, I don't see why *I* should hurry. I've got much more than that *already*.

At the Quay. – People in Oban stare a good deal. Can't quite make out reason, unless they're surprised to find me up so early. Explain that I got up without having even been called. Oban populace mildly surprised, and offer me neckties – *Why?*

Fine steamer this; has a paddle-wheel at *both* ends – 'because,' the Captain explains, 'she has not only to *go* to Gairloch – but come back as well.'

First-rate navigator, the Captain; he has written my weight, the date of my last birth-day, and the number of the house I live in, down in a sort of ledger he keeps. He does this with all his passengers, he tells me, reduces the figures to logarithms, and works out the ship's course in decimals. No idea there was so much science in modern sea-manship.

On Board. – Great advantage of being so early is that you can breakfast quietly on deck before starting. Have mine on bridge of steamer, under awning; everything very good – ham-méringues *excellent*. No coffee, but, instead, a capital brand of dry sparkling marmalade, served, sailor-fashion, in small pomatum-pots.

What a small world we live in! Of all people in the world, who should be sitting next to me but my AUNT MARIA! I was always under the impression that she had died in my infancy. Don't like to mention this, because if I am *wrong*, she might be offended. But if she *did* die when I was a child she ought to be a much older woman than she looks. I *do* tell her this – because it is really a compliment.

My Aunt, evidently an experienced trav-eller, never travels, she informs me, without a pair of globes and a lawn-mower. She offers, very kindly, to lend me the Celestial globe, if the weather is at all windy. This is behaving *like* an Aunt!

We are taking in live-stock; curious-looking creatures, like spotted pug-dogs (only bigger and woollier, of course) and without horns. Somebody leaning over the rail, next to me (I *think* he is the Public Prosecutor, but am not quite sure), tells me they are 'Scotch Shortbreads'. Agreeable man, but rather given to staring.

Didn't observe it before, but my Aunt is really amazingly like GLADSTONE. Ask her to explain this. She is much distressed that I have noticed it; says she has felt it coming on for some time; it is not, as she justly complains, as if she took any interest in poli-tics either. She has consulted every doctor in London, and they all tell her it is simply weakness, and she will outgrow it with care. Singular case – must find out (delicately) whether it's catching.

We ought to be starting soon; feel quite fresh and lively, in spite of having got up so early. Mention this to Captain. Wish he and the Public Prosecutor wouldn't stare at me so. Just as if there was something singular in my appearance!

They're embarking my portmanteau now. Knew they would have a lively time of it! It takes, at least, four sailors, in kilts, to manage it. Ought I to step ashore and quiet it down? Stay where I am. Don't know why, but feel a little afraid of it when it's like this. Shall exchange it for a quiet hand-bag when I get home.

Captain busy hammering at a hole in the funnel – dangerous place to spring a leak in – hope he is making it watertight. The hammering reminds me of that poor devil in the bedroom next to mine at the Hotel. *He* won't catch the boat now – he *can't!* My Aunt (who has left off looking like Mr GLAD-STONE) asks me why I am laughing. I tell her about that unfortunate man and his 'thirty-five seconds'. She screams with laughter. Very humorous woman, my Aunt.

Deck crowded with passengers now: all pointing and staring ... at whom? Ask Aunt MARIA. She declines to tell me: says, severely, that, 'If I don't know, I ought to.'

Great Heavens! it's at *me* they're staring! And no wonder – in the hurry I was in, I must have packed *everything* up! ... I've come away just as I was! *Now* I understand why someone offered me a necktie. Where shall I go and hide myself? Shall I ever persuade that beast of a portmanteau to give me out one or two things to put on – because I really *can't* go about like this! Captain still hammering at funnel – but he can't wake that sleepy-headed idiot in the next room. 'Louder – knock *louder*, or the boat will go without him! Tell him there isn't another for two days. He's said good-bye to everybody he knows at Oban – he will look such an ass if he doesn't go, after all!' ... Not the least use! Wonder what his name is. My Aunt says *she* knows, only she won't tell me – she'll whisper it, as a great secret. She is just about to disclose the name, which, somehow, I am extremely curious to know – when ...

Where am I? Haven't they got that unhappy fellow up *yet*? Why the dickens are they knocking at *my* door? I've been on board the steamer for hours, I tell you! Eh? *what*? Five minutes to eight! And the Gairloch boat? 'Sailed at usual time – seven. Tried to make you hear – but couldn't.' ... Confound it all! Good mind not to get up all day – now!

27.10.1888

*'First-class passengers always get
the de luxe burial.'*

'I always wish I'd gone into the navy. I just revel in the life at sea.'

PONT.

The Heiress Falls Overboard.

'I'll be sorry when he leaves home – he's such a damn good navigator.'

Alan Brien

TUSCAN COLUMNS

The Shelley party, like most English travellers of their tastes and class for the next hundred years, actively preferred Italy as their favourite foreign country at any time of the year – so long as it wasn't summer. The Roman spring, Venice in the autumn, even winter in Florence or Naples, these provided paradisal exile for successive trendy Tuscan Sets of their era. Only the brazen, importunate sun, in the days before refrigeration, beach undress, air-conditioning and rapid, comfortable transport, as it boiled the pallid, tepid-blooded Anglo-Saxons alive at noon, ensured that July and August for them was a season in hell.

To be exact, Percy Bysshe himself, eccentric and pioneer in this as in so many other things, had fits of what seemed to the rest a perverse appetite for solar heat. During the summer of 1819, he set up his household in a farmhouse-cum-villa on a hill outside Livorno, attracted particularly by the multi-windowed balcony on its roof that he called his 'glass tower'. To everyone else, his wife Mary later recalled, just to enter this light-house was 'intolerable', but Shelley 'basked' here, pretending he was afloat in one of his imagined airships, watching the waterspouts chase each other across the Ligurian Sea, revivified by a sauna for both body and mind.

When the sun still blazed at the end of September, even Shelley swore off the heat-fixes which kept him on a perpetual high, and set off with the eight-month pregnant Mary, and his ever-loving sister-in-law Claire, to winter in Florence. Here they stayed through the bright, sharp, dry weather that lasted into the New Year, the heavy falls of snow in mid-January, the city's harshest freeze for 70 years, departing at the end of the month when the thaw bathed Florence in long hours of mild warmth.

On my own way to the region for Christmas and New Year, I could not resist turning to some old notes on the Romantics Abroad, unopened for decades. Their journey from Pisa to Florence, stopping over for the night at Empoli, took them two days in a rattling unsprung carriage. On their return, via the fastest conveyance there-abouts known to man, an Arno river-boat with an icy, fol-lowing east wind, they took nine hours at what must have seemed a dizzying speed.

I started off, like many air travellers to Florence, slightly indignant that even the national carrier, Alitalia, does not have a city airport there to decant you within a taxi ride. Instead, it off-loads you at Pisa.

But, unlike our own British Rail link at Gatwick, or even the London Transport interchange at Heathrow, airport and station are within anybody's definition of two min-utes' walk – and what's more, on the flat, with ticket desks, baggage deposit or retrieval, left luggage, information for the two services,

cheek by jowl with an ever-open bar. And the train from Pisa to Florence now runs to coincide with the flights, taking less than an hour. It almost makes you ashamed not to be a poet – what other excuses have you for what you did with the time you saved?

It was battling his way along the banks of the Arno, weaving through the riverside forests, in the teeth of growing Christmas gales, that Shelley was inspired to write his *Ode to the West Wind*. You might have thought it more likely to have had its imagery and its impact from his view from the wrap-around eyrie near Livorno. But then you cannot have experienced the way the air in Florence whistles around you, often sim-ultaneously from north, south, east and west, once the sun has finished its tour of inspec-tion for the day. Much of the place never sees the sun in its dank, dark depths whatever the season of the year.

The streets of Florence, notably those radiating clockwise from the Duomo round to the Arno and along to the Ponte Vecchio, are much narrower, more crooked and more random in their twists, but above all lined with much taller buildings, than most of us either expect or indeed remember. They form a linked web of grandiose alleys, looped with piazzas, knotted by palaces which are flung high on a massive scale for some secur-ity and ostentation that is beyond a canny, bourgeois English imagining.

Houses, shops, factories, warehouses, tiers of flats – one short block often combining the lot behind a single façade – are also reared up on a giant scale compared to any English equivalent. The doors are exhibited in daz-zling variety, rising to the height of a couple of our old London storeys, fitted out as stan-dard with great pillars, porticoes, canopics, tympana, lunettes, architraves, worthy of a moderate Chicago bank or gargantuan Dublin slum.

Past every two or three of even these over-powering entrances, it is commonplace to find that the way-in to some quite modest nest of recessed apartments has huge castle gates leading on to a flag-stoned, arched-ceiling, stained-glass lodge that might appear a trifle elaborate for an Oxbridge college.

The windows that are framed along these canyon walls also exhibit a scale that dwarfs anything of the kind we see in our buildings of the same periods. All of them, everywhere, whether hung along main streets or back tracks, whether accessible to intruders on the lower floors or isolated in blank masonry near the roof, like outlets for cranes, are without exception knitted over with fretted ironwork grilles. You might expect these to seem oppressive or threatening, as though you had wandered into a presentation of 'Security Through The Ages' at the International Ideal Gaol Exhibition. Instead, they become attractive *al fresco* furniture, no more connected to actualities, or fantasies, of riot and ransacking than the token walled front gardens of the inner London village or the complex, many-armed locks on the gates of a London square.

These historic and memorable warrens, thanks to *turismo* brilliantly lit until the early hours, cleared of garbage every day of the year, and almost certainly safer to walk than the thoroughfares of any other world famous city (except perhaps Moscow) do act as a cosmic changing-post of the winds. Even the most ardent Florentophile must admit that there is barely a moment in winter when the air is not rushing from one corner to the next and back again, round and round the square, in a restless game of tag.

We had borrowed a third-floor, two-room flat in one of the oldest quarters, behind the Teatro Verdi, across the road from Santa Croce. We were within five minutes' walk of more antique statues, wall-size Old Masters, vistas of umber and gold and sepia perspectives, marble squares and terracotta towers, fortresses that could have been chipped out of old cork, Babylonian roof gardens, cavernous apothecary's shops like Etruscan temples, pavements hand-laid in individually baked bricks, than would seem convincing if we had been born, and raised, in the British Museum. Yet the other city in which I have lived that came to mind on waking each morning was New York.

As your eyes opened the light filtered down from above, bouncing, bending, taking on tints and shades as it sank, like a shower of glass rods in an aquarium. It was worse than guesswork to estimate the cold of the sky and the state of the weather from the pattern on the window. Even leaning out, and squinting up, was little help unless you could spot a small geometrical shape of sunshine far away among the chimney tops.

The contrast between eternally chilly depths and gradually warmed externals may be what keeps the winds on their toes. Certainly, hardly a Florentine is to be seen unprotected by the impervious, malleable armour of some other creature's skin. The women are all in furs, the men all in leather. After a few days during which the cover dropped on the parrot's cage, bringing with it the boisterous, blood-chilling dark, around four in the afternoon, I began to regard the citizens less with righteous disapproval than with selfish envy.

There seemed to be no occasion, inside almost as often as outside, where the fur coat did not rate as regular wear. I saw women bicycling in furs, usually in the wrong direction down a one-way street and into the pedestrian precinct. (In Italy, the bike has all the rights of a citizen on foot and ignores traffic laws for vehicles. But then, at least in Naples and the south, I was solemnly informed that the red light was not an order to anybody but more in the way of a bit of friendly advice.) I saw women in furs cutting up fish in the market, carrying loads of newspapers into shops, sweeping out courtyards, breast-feeding the baby on the bus.

What I did not notice, in my glazed male way, was that the fur coat was a many-patterned uniform, regimented according to rank. Once you had learned the signs, you could identify the class of every Florentine female. This was demonstrated to me by a city resident of cosmopolitan origin. Wherever we were, she would say something like – 'See, that is the daughter. She is wearing the top level working-class fur. But she is with her mother-in-law who demonstrates her dominance by wearing the bottom level middle-class fur.'

The leather of the attendant male kept pace, though in rather more subtle fashion which it took me longer to spot, usually restricting the fur to a lining. An exception was pointed out in the Via de Tornabuoni, a shopping arcade commonly described as 'the Bond Street of Florence' though, to me, a dedicated non-shopper, it seemed far superior as a theatrical show-case, a display of conspicuous commercialism presented with electrifying style.

Here were a couple, probably in their late sixties, identically dressed in a soft, neat patchwork of pinky-grey fur from high-collared neck to Gucci bootees, heads topped with fluffy turbans of the same dead creatures. My guide estimated they were carrying on their backs the price of a sizeable luxury flat, probably in the Tornabuoni. And so did every other passer-by. Which was the point of the exercise.

Italy, I always forget, is a society almost as dominated by bureaucracy as the Soviet Union. It is now against the law for those providing a variety of services to fail to insist on giving a *ricevuta*, or formal receipt, to the customer. It is now even against the law for the customer, receiving the services, to fail to insist on being given the *ricevuta*. No Italian (well, no Florentine that I met) would dream of going anywhere, except backwards and forwards to work, without a *marco di bolla*, an official stamped document, a 'bull' as in Papal bull, priced from 700 lire up to 5000 lire (say 25p to £3). This is rather like a sworn affidavit in Britain and is used to make legal and binding hundreds of transactions which elsewhere might pass on a nod and a handshake.

This is not because the Italians like paperwork or are obsessively legalistic. Quite the contrary, they wish to avoid altogether any connection with authority, particularly paying taxes, an enforced tribute that a lifetime of Fascism and inefficient, corrupt postwar governments has taught them goes more often into private pockets than public coffers. No self-employed persons reveal more than a fraction of their income to the state, brazenly declaring disposable assets only half those of their house-keeper or gardener. The weekly-waged alone stump up the correct amount, so that official statistics can declare Fiat car-workers the nation's top earners. Hence the *marco di bolla* and the *ricevuta* which are the Government's way of creaming off a little from the black economy. Last year, there was an attempt to impose the receipt system on all shops. But the shopkeepers came out on strike and, after two days, the measure was cancelled.

One of the rewards of Italy in the winter, especially if you holiday there in a flat rather than a hotel, and cook for yourselves from the rich treasures of market produce, is that you can at least kid yourselves you are temporary Florentines rather than tourist outsiders.

By the time our Alitalia plane banked over the wrinkled sea out of Pisa, giving us a far glimpse of Lerici, where Shelley ate his last meal before sailing into the storm from which he returned a half-eaten corpse and where really we enjoyed our 1984 Christmas seafood lunch, leaving behind a Florence where we attended mass at the Duomo on Christmas Eve and had drinks at the Communist Casa di Popolo on New Year's Eve, I felt that our short winter trip to Italy had bonded us far more strongly to that beautiful, exciting, irritating country than any long summer vacation.

23.1.1985

'I'm sorry, Henry, but I'm leaving you. Giorgio was sympathetic about the pound and I was concerned for the lira and one thing led to another.'

Julian Barnes

ON THE TERRACE

A Short Story

They sat on the terrace with their backs to a wafting spray of plumbago and watched the head waiter. Now, ten years on, he was plumper, balder, a little brusquer than when they had first come. Guiltless accomplices, they waited for his first victim of the evening.

He was called Victor – Monsieur Victor to the staff and most of the guests – and he never touched a plate. He received customers with a sideways inclination of the head – assessing them rather than indicating defer-

ence – and after a brief scrutiny conducted them to the table he judged appropriate to their status and pretensions. Favoured clients in soft casual clothes were assigned to the front tables overlooking the lake; new money in white shoes and sun-glasses was displayed in the centre of the terrace; foreigners, gawky lovers and brash youths were placed at the edge of things.

Then he took your order. Whatever you chose, it seemed to confirm his opinion of you. Dick, who normally stuck to vermouth, had once asked for a vodka and citron pressé. Victor's expression hadn't flickered, but Dick immediately felt that the waiter knew everything about him, from the turmoil of his deposit account to the way his vests unpicked at the armpits; knew, too, that Dick had never dared order such a drink before.

'Look, what about *them*,' Christine suddenly whispered. Dick wished she hadn't. For him, part of the fun was watching Victor's act without comment and guessing the victims for yourself.

'Perhaps.'

'Oh, but I'm *sure*,' his wife came back brightly, spoiling the game again. 'Surey-*sure*.'

Victor had arrived at a table a few yards away to collect the bill. It was not up to you to decide when you paid; it was up to Victor. He appeared at your table and, scarcely bending at all, lowered a silver tray towards you. You laid your money and the bill on it (Victor would never pick anything off the table himself); the tray would be withdrawn while Victor compared the two items on it, then would return, from its celestial source, with your change. It was held in position for a few seconds while you decided on your tip.

The table Christine had pointed out contained a quartet of Italianate youths who had hung raucously over cheap drinks. Victor's tray had just been hauled up for the second time, and Dick realised, with a mixture of pleasure and irritation, that his wife's guess had been correct. Victor stood completely still for about ten seconds, staring at the tip that had been left. Then he turned towards the main body of the terrace and with a twitch of the head alerted his black-suited waiters; they froze in what they were doing, and watched him. This sudden unavailability of waiters ensured that some of the customers watched as well.

Victor gave each of the four youths an impassive, two-second glance (one of them was already reaching uneasily into his trouser pocket), then extended his arm full out in front of him – as if the contents of his tray were certainly malodorous if not positively infectious – and marched towards the edge of the terrace. Everyone was watching him now. At the low wall he paused, turned for a final accusing stare at the offending table, and contemptuously deposited the tip into the lake. Then, head up, the tray held close to the side-stripe of his black trousers, he walked quickly back into the hotel.

'If there's one thing I can't stand in a man,' commented Christine in what Dick thought of as her Domesday Book voice, 'it's meanness.'

Dick didn't have any trouble understanding what she said; he had, after all, heard her say the same thing before. But he wondered idly what the precise focus of Christine's reflection was: the behaviour of the Italians; Victor's gesture; the general moral condition of mankind; or, just possibly, the occasion ten years ago when a slimmer Victor had tipped into the lake Dick's own first, hesitating attempt to calculate eight per cent.

'They did look a bit rough, didn't they, dear?' was what he replied.

'They?' The tone was puzzled, slightly condescending.

'Those Eyeties.'

'Oh, yes.'

'Who were you thinking about?'

'Oh, you know,' Christine gave a little shrug and gestured out across the terrace towards the lake, 'the *beau idéal*.' She gave a false laugh. It was the laugh that meant, Don't mind me with my silly thoughts, Don't mind me with my silly, yearning, ungraspable nature.

Dick wondered why his wife never used French phrases in England.

'I like the way he does it,' he said in a slow, pacifying tone. Christine looked across at him as if examining the price tag on a dress. 'I mean, I thought it showed real ...' He was going to say *panache*, but substituted, '... style.'

'I suppose so.'

'The bit I like best is where he turns round and catches the other waiters' attention. It's as if he's saying, You can insult me with your mean little tip, I'm above that sort of thing; but don't insult my friends, my brothers, my children. Something like that. Real style.'

'Yes, you could say he's got *panache*,' Christine offered conciliatingly. Even so, Dick sensed that something was still wrong.

Christine was silent.

'Is it something, dear?'

'Oh, no.' Less than a shrug.

'Sure? Surey-sure?'

'Oh well, Dick, you know . . . I hardly like to bring things up on our second honeymoon. Serious things . . . I suppose I think it should be as much like the first as possible. Only that isn't possible, really, is it? No, I was just having a *rêverie* . . . I suppose it struck me as typical, Dick, that you were interested in the way Victor did his act, and I was more interested in the, the wider conclusions one might draw from that little *mise en scène*.'

Dick wondered why she called him Dick when he was only two feet away and she couldn't be addressing anyone else. Then he wondered if that wasn't exactly the sort of thing she was complaining about anyway.

'*Au fond*,' she went on, 'I suppose I'm more interested in the essence of things, and you're more interested in the surfaces. I think that's one of the things I've discovered since I got married. Don't get me wrong, Dick; I'm not dishing out brownie points or anything. I'm simply making an observation.'

'Do you think he's going to do it again?' Dick asked, with false interest, deliberately breaking his own rules.

Ten years ago they had first come to the terrace as a treat. Dick had just started in data processing; they couldn't afford the hotel, and were staying at an auberge up in the hills. After Dick's first tip had disappeared into the lake they had gone back and had dinner, laughed over several glasses of Calvados, and gone to bed. The next evening they had returned to the terrace and the level of Dick's tipping had been judged appropriate. Someone else's, however, had not; and this amused them.

'How much do you think they lose?' Chris-tine had asked him that night as they were leaving.

'They gain.'

'What do you mean?'

'They gain,' he merely repeated. In those days he used to enjoy his didactic opportunities.

'How? How?'

'Because everyone puts in a bit more once they see it happening to someone else.'

In the scented dusk he felt his forearm being pressed a little more tightly. That's right, the bridal squeeze seemed to say, Of course, *that*'s what husbands are for: to tell you things; to know things. That's why you marry them.

Ten years on Dick didn't find his arm being pressed in quite the same way any more. Instead he felt that Christine knew more things now than he did. Or rather, he felt that she believed she knew more things than he did. Once, the world had been full of his elucidations; now it was full of her generalisations. Dick wondered how this had come about. After all, she hadn't exactly sat around reading encyclopaedias.

One morning after breakfast, Dick found himself at their window, staring out at the lake and musing about all the money Victor had tipped into it over the years. As he stood there, the water seemed to become bluer, cleaner, warmer; he saw the glitter of sun on its surface, and then from below a solider, fiercer glitter of coins. He passed through the surface and his vision immediately cleared, as if he were wearing a diver's mask. The coins, he could now see, were larger than he thought, clean and golden, uncon-taminated by time or water. Pieces of eight. They lay casually on a shelf of tropical coral; a shoal of fish swayed past like the shimmy of a model's dress on a softly lit catwalk. Everything was warm and calm.

'Shall we go here, Dick?' Christine was still in bed, with half a croissant balanced on the pillow and Michelin map 84 spread out along the ridge of her knees.

'Where?'

'Here.' She jabbed at the map without looking up. Dick didn't move.

'All right.'

Christine folded up the map. Why couldn't he be bothered to come over? Why did she have to suggest everything twice? There were times when Dick seemed downright provoking; either that or plain facetious. Yesterday, for instance, they'd driven to Eze, and walked up streets full of potters and craftsmen to that strange cactus-covered hilltop. As they gazed over the corrugated terracotta roof-tiles to the cliffs and the sea beyond, she'd said, harmlessly enough, she thought, 'It's just like a picture postcard.'

Dick's reply had been a grunt. They'd walked down through the cacti again and stopped in a tourists' shop. She'd picked out a few pleasant views of the village and held them in a fan in front of him. She was being friendly, but he'd only grunted and said, 'Looks just like a picture postcard.'

Had she been meant to laugh, or what? That was just like Dick nowadays. Almost as if he were testing you. Why should he want to do a thing like that after all these years? It was like the other evening, when she'd passed a remark about how pretty the plumbago was looking. He just replied, 'It was Cecil Rhodes's favourite flower.'

That was all. No indication of whether he approved Cecil Rhodes's taste in flora (and her own, incidentally), or whether he was using the preference of one to disparage the other. And then she found herself thinking, how come he knew *that*? He wasn't interested in flowers; he didn't care about Africa. He wouldn't have come across that sort of thing in newspapers, or in the naval histories he was so keen on. *Why* did he know something like that, she reflected irritably. And why did he know *that*, as opposed to knowing different things, useful things?

Still, Christine thought, you couldn't say they didn't get on. Dick had to be chivvied a bit, but he'd always been a good provider. And you had to feel slightly sorry for men, anyway; for the way they didn't develop; for the way they weren't so close to the children. *And* Dick's hair was going grey over his ears. *And* he'd have to go to the oculist soon. When they were walking up to Eze, she'd pointed out a blur of smoke on the horizon and asked him where he thought it was bound for.

'I can't see it,' he said.

'Sure?' she'd asked, 'Surey-sure? There. Just there.' She leaned on his shoulder and stretched out her arm to guide his eyes.

'I think I need glasses,' he said. She had pressed his arm in a quick, firm, sympathetic squeeze. The sort of squeeze, Dick imagined, which a nurse might give you if you were dying.

On the final evening of their holiday, they dined near the middle of the terrace. Twice now Victor had awarded them this grudging promotion.

'Dick,' Christine murmured over the hors d'oeuvre, and he followed her eye to where a rigid Victor was about to expose the meanness of a pair of plump, olive-suited businessmen. Dick merely nodded, and they watched the performance together in silence. But it was an amiable silence; while Christine liked to maintain that every meal – even when they were just *à deux* – was a social occasion, she wasn't inflexible. She didn't mind this silence. She reached under the table and rested the toe of her shoe against his ankle, as a way of telling him so.

The night took over; Victor and his staff brought oil lamps to the more favoured tables. Later, Dick sat over his brandy while Christine, pulling her shawl more tightly round her shoulders, gazed out at the lake. You couldn't really see the water except when it moved; if it stayed completely still, no one would know it was there.

She thought about all the tips that had gone into the lake over the last ten years. She tried estimating the average bad tip, and then multiplying by – what? – three thousand? But would the same amount get thrown in all the year round? She didn't know. Instead, she imagined what it would be like if all the money stayed where it fell: a great reef of small change, made larger every day by Victor's instructive additions. After a few years it would bulge up above the surface of the lake; the centimes and francs would rattle with the tug of water like pebbles on a beach.

But Christine knew it didn't happen like that. The coins were too light; they wouldn't stay where they fell. After an hour, a day, undercurrents would ripple them loose, drag them off, dump them in some mud-filled pothole in a distant part of the lake. Everything would get dispersed, inevitably. At the thought of this she felt a sharp melancholy. She took her toe away from her husband's ankle, and realised that her calf muscle had stiffened up in the cold.

'Dick, darling, let's go in. Early start tomorrow.'

But the next day, a Sunday, they were not the first to rise. Jean-Marie, the hotel's most junior employee, a *plongeur* with ambitions to own a café, was woken by Victor just as it was getting light. On Saturday nights Jean-Marie slept in his swimming trunks. He put his dressing-gown on and followed the head waiter down to the terrace. Victor handed him the goggles, then the circular plastic box with a hole in the lid. He knotted a rope round the boy's waist and helped lower him over the retaining wall of the terrace.

The late summer water was cool, and Jean-Marie worked quickly. Victor always dropped the money at the same point, and immediately below it one of Jean-Marie's predecessors – perhaps even the young Victor himself – had helpfully scooped out a bowl-shaped depression. Most of the coins were still shiny; those he had missed the previous week were already acquiring a greenish tinge. The *plongeur* transferred everything he found to the plastic box, explored around him for a few feet, then surfaced and hauled himself up the rope. He gave the box to Victor, who patted him on the shoulder. A hot shower and back to bed. After everyone else had risen, Mme Victor would reward him with breakfast on a tray.

Soon it would be autumn and the lake would be getting colder. Victor said that he would only have to go down once a fortnight then; possibly, if it was really cold and custom was slack, only every three weeks. Even so, Jean-Marie wasn't sure he'd stick the job.

28.10.1981

Laurie Taylor

CULTURE VULTURE SHOCK

'I'm sorry, Geoff, but let's get this crystal clear. Are you accusing me of actually *saying* that? You're saying that I *said* that?'

'I don't know about you *saying* it, but you certainly implied as much.'

'Look, Geoff, don't give me "implied". A minute ago you said "said". That's a very different matter from "implied", isn't it?'

'Well, you as good as *said* it. Put it like that.'

'No, I'm sorry, Geoff. You've gone a little too far this time. I want to hear what other people think about all this. Put it to the vote. Did anyone here – anyone at all in our group – ever hear me say that Jacopo Tintoretto was without doubt the supreme Renaissance colourist? Did anyone ever hear me say that?'

Although there were eight of us sitting around the table at the well-located Pensione Salute, dipping our after-dinner grapes in the now pleasantly tepid bowl of water, not one of us could quite remember Alex coming out with those exact words.

'What I *did* say, and it was on about the second day of last year's holiday, just after we'd been bargaining with that man outside the Accademia about the price of the melon slices – "*cocomero*", remember? – what I said, then, was that Tintoretto was arguably the Renaissance master of *chiaroscuro*, of light and shade, that is. Light and shade. Right, Geoff? Not colour. There is a difference, you know.'

You could feel that the atmosphere was becoming charged, and although most of us were still in a contented mood after a fine meal of minestrone, liver (Venetian style), and *zuppa inglese*, I, for one, was pleased that Christine stopped peeling her grapes for a second and tried to introduce some sense of proportion into the proceedings.

'Look, do stop it, you two. I mean, what's the point of falling out over details, over who said exactly what, and to whom. We're all Tintoretto people, aren't we?'

I could see that her appeal had got through to Geoff. He switched his eyes away from Alex and took a large reflective sip from his *acqua minerale* glass.

'I mean, everybody here recognises that Tintoretto's footsteps are all over Venice and that the sheer power and vitality of his imagination was unparalleled by any of his contemporaries. Yes?'

'Yes,' muttered Geoff.

'And surely everyone here would agree that he worked like a giant, flinging himself "upon the wings of all the winds"?'

Most of us nodded.

'So why, for goodness sake, spoil the evening with such pointless bickering?'

Of course, in a way, it was easy for Christine to talk. Not only had she steered clear of the Barolo that evening because such heavy red wine tended to aggravate her mosquito bites, but she'd also been in the South Manchester Tintoretto group ever since that rainy day at the Lido back in 1976 when a small group of people sheltering together in a tiny beach-hut had decided to do something in their own way to counter Paul Theroux's interesting but sweeping generalisation that 'travel, so broadening at first' eventually 'contracts the mind'.

Compared to Christine, Alex and Geoff were virtual newcomers to cultural vacations: Alex coming over to us from a primarily Oldham-based Carpaccio group in 1983 when he felt it was taking a slightly too sentimental view of Gentile Bellini, and Geoff only deserting the Didsbury Titian society in 1984 after a ridiculous argument one night in St Mark's Square about the exact symbolic significance of the old woman with the eggs in the *Presentation*.

'Look, do me a favour, Christine.' Whatever Geoff's view of the matter it was instantly clear that Alex was anxious to return to the fray. 'No one needs your help. Our friend Geoff here is positively looking for a little aggro. Am I right, Geoffrey?'

'I don't know what you're talking about. I really don't. I only took up a remark which you yourself made less than twelve months ago . . .'

'I think you do, old son. I think you do. I've been watching you very carefully this holiday. There have been little signs. Last Monday, for example, when you slipped out of San Rocco just as we were getting down to some detailed work on the top left hand corner of *Paradiso*.'

'Only because I had to get some antihistamine before the chemist's . . .'

'And then on Tuesday I caught you giggling in front of *Cain and Abel*.'

'Well, there is something a little disconcerting about the way they're . . .'

'And now there's all this chunter about the significance of colour. What next, Geoffrey, old boy? A few casual references to the distinctive qualities of *The Madonna of the Pesaro*?'

Even in the candlelight it was clear that Geoff had started to blush at Alex's reference.

'I don't know what you're talking about,' he blurted, clumsily tipping the dregs of the *acqua minerale* bottle into his *grappa* glass.

'Or perhaps *The Frari Assumption*?'

'I've never mentioned the merits of *The Frari Assumption* in your presence, and you know it.'

'I'm on to you, Geoffrey Tremlett. Oh yes, although you've been sitting around with us for the last two weeks, licking your chocolate *gelati*, sipping your lemon *spremutas*, and going on like everyone else about how the lavish power with which Tintoretto treats every subject cannot but fail to impress the beholder, you haven't changed your spots at all. I know where your loyalty lies. You're still a Titian man.'

'I admit there *are* certain things that he did well. I mean, most experts would agree that his power of portraiture was unsurpassed.'

'Don't give me "certain things that he did well". *Titian*? Are we talking about Titian? Then perhaps you'd be so good as to tell me who it was who turned the young Tintoretto out of his studio? Who it was who threw this 15-year-old raw genius on to the streets whence he was forced to search out each and every occasion for the exercise of his prodigious talent?'

'That's out of order, Alex, and you damned well know it. Tintoretto was far from blameless in the encounter. The dyer's son was often carried away by the violence and extravagance of his own imagination, by, in a word, his *spirito stravagante*.'

'A "violence and extravagance", which you know only too well, Geoffrey Tremlett, was the driving force behind such acknowledged masterpieces as *Moses Receiving the Tablets of the Law* and *The Last Judgement*.'

'It's a pity, then, that for all their mastery of composition, such pictures singularly fail to convey any profound sense of human feeling or compassion across the centuries.'

'I'm sorry, Geoff, but that's the last straw. That's it. Quite enough for one day. Let's settle this outside.'

'Oh, that's fine. Nothing you old Carpaccio people like better than simple narrative solutions to transcendental issues.'

'OUTSIDE.'

'RIGHT.'

It was a thoroughly nasty moment, one indeed which might have marred our entire cultural vacation, had not Christine, at that very moment, spotted through the blinds a group of youths making their way down our *calle*.

'Geoff. Alex. Everybody,' she whispered, putting her hand over the water bowl to block off the distraction of the remaining grapes. 'Outside. By the pleasantly quiet small canal. It's the Giorgione mob.'

That was more than enough for most of us. We were on our feet in an instant, and with Alex bawling 'quasi-mystical bastards' at the top of his voice, and Geoff leading us all in a chorus of 'Here We Go', we chased them half a mile along the Fondamenta to Ruskin's House where, with a pleasantly renewed sense of our own solidarity, we linked arms and chanted '*Raphael, Raphael*,' outside the proprietor's window until it was time for bed.

15.1.1986

Alan Coren

THE HEATHROW TALES

that Aprille with his taxe-
formes drere
Comes, draggynge in a new fynancial yeere,
Thenne many folke loke round to see how
theye
May kepe the Inlande Revenue atte baye;
And hardly has the litel month begunne
Thanne journalystes start trekkinge to the
sunne,
To write of places off the beaten trackes,
And sette expenses off agaynst thir taxe:
A pilgrimage, in shorte, not for thir soules,
But (as it is wyth modern mankynde's
goales)
To keepe a few bob backe. Thus, did I
wende
To Heathrowe, there my further steppes to
bende
Towards some sunsoked costa; and I founde
The spotte was thikke wyth pilgrims! All
arounde
They milled and chattered, singlie and in
groupes;
And everywhere, the bright emblazon'd
troops
Of Travail Agents hopped and chyrped like
sparrowes,
Dyspensing labels, poyntinge uppe at
arrowes,

Dyscharging these to Lourdes, and those to
Rome,
And others who were off to see the home
Inne wich Lorde Byron lived, or John
Keates died,
Or Wolfgang Amadeus Mozart cryed
When (being seven) his Daddye would not
lette
Him staye uppe to compose a stringe
quartette.
And yette, for all the bustle and the cryes,
Not one soule saw I takynge to the skyes,
And eek my own flyte no man came to call;
We merely mobbed the grate departure hall
And gayzed uppe at the indicator-bord,
For such bleeke gleenings as it would afforde
Of flytes not inne, not oute, not onne, not
knowne,
Of strykes and goe-slowes; and muche else
(not showne)
Like drunken crewes, lost rear doors, and
the sounde
Of tickynge baggage, kept us onne the
grounde.

Thus was it thatte it came aboute by chance
As we poore pilgrims trodde our loanly
dance
Upon the Heathrowe tiles, thatte one of us
(Drop't there two dayes bifor by airporte
bus)
Suggested thatte we wile aware the time
With tales thatte each wold tell the reste, in
ryme!
We clap't, we cheer'd, our weery eyes grew
bryte;
We sang the praises of thatte worthie wight!
Then satte we downe, wyth whiskey, beere,
and gin,
And wayted for the firste one to biginne.
But lette me, whyle I have the tyme and
space,
Ere thatte I ferther in this storie pace,
Sette downe the manere of thatte companye,
And wich they weren, and of what degree;
And eek in what array thatte they were inne!
And at a clericke wol I firste biginne.

A BISHOPPE hadde we wyth us in thatte
    place,
A slimme yung manne whose bryte and
    beerdlesse face
Glowed wyth a pinkish-white cherubicke
    hue,
Broughte on in parte by prayer, but most by
    Brut.
This worthie manne had turned his
    mohaired backe
Upon the easeful parishe life: no hacke
For Christ was he, to pat the wrinkled hande
Of borynge widowes, or each weeke to
    stande
Inne some raine-sodden pulpytte, there to
    speeke
Some low-paid sermon to the grottie meeke.
Westward he turned his course, towardes
    those isles
Where heathen soules pursued those living-
    stiles
Thatte frighte the Christian; where the idle
    rich
Have found atte laste a litel taxe-free niche
Whereinne to set thir golden calves; to
    pounce
Whenne golde goes up to ninety-five an
    ounce,
And where, to ease thir soules, they ofte
    invite
The better class of prieste to spende the
    nyghte;
Or three months, if the truth were told. So
    thatte
They ease thir conscience, as we worm a
    catte.
The prieste in his turn, for the boone thus
    given,
Makes sure the taxe-evaded soule is shriven,
And coming home all tanned, white teeth a-
    gleem,
Turns out for cricket wyth his village
    teeme –
Hee fyndes the countryside the place to
    dwell;
For theologians writing *What Is Hell?*
(A six-part series for the *Sunday Tymes*)

Need peace and quiet; rural life, too, chimes
Wyth tearynge uppe to towne one day a
    weeke
So thatte the national presse may heer him
    speeke
His piece on porno in the House of Lordes,
Or rayle on telly about Christian frauds.

Biside him satte a NOVELISTE, al pale,
Who once, tenne yeeres bifor, had writ a tale
So true, so deepe, so geered to thisse darke
    age
Thatte, ere the reeder turned the final page,
He knew *Roome Atte The Botom* was the one
To acte on Eng. Lit. lyke the mornynge
    sunne,
Who sheddes his warmynge beemes on
    soggie soyle
To maturate the plottes where seedlynges
    toyle.
Thus, al arounde, we saw the seedlynges
    bask;
The noveliste, meenwile, clove to his taske,
And lo! Ere yet a litel yeere had trip't
He hadde terned out a stunnynge movie
    scripte
Based onne the boke. It won sixteene
    awardes
(And, naturally, reeped other fatte rewardes:
The noveliste moved to the South of
    France).
The nexte yeere saw a wonderful new dance,
The Botom (fromme the musical), by wich
The noveliste now waxed exceedynge rich.
And still the grate creative juices flow'd!
For, after thatte, thisse noveliste now
    show'd
How righte *Roome Atte The Botom* prov'd
    to bee
In ninety-seven parts on ITV.
Whereat this prodygal son of his tyme
Turned his unrestynge hande to
    pantomime:
*Roome Atte The Botom Meets Dick
    Whittington*
(Wyth Tomie Steele and Twiggie) was put
    on

Atte the Palladium. It ranne and ranne!
Was there no stoppynge thisse creative
   manne?
Alas! His ice showe flop't. His Muse, for
   once,
Now founde her litel lyre reft of stunts.
And now, with tenne yeeres gone, the
   noveliste
Muste needes revyve. And his psychiatriste
Together wyth his agente and, of course,
His thirde wife, feel a visyte to the source
Of his firste inspiration mighte wel loose
His writer's block; and – who can tel? –
   produce
Downe Atte The Botom, or some other sequel
Whose spynne-off possibilities mighte equal
The pickynges of the firste. So here todaye
He goes in serche of Ernest Hemingwaye
(Whose nice short werdes our man always
   admir'd:
The hand, with polysyllables, growes tired);
He trekkes to Paris, thence to Rome, and
   soon
Will lie benceth Pamplona's risynge moon
And fille his dreggy cuppe at thatte fresshe
   spring
Where Papa roared, biside the bloodstayned
   ring.
But things are not quyte alwayes as they
   seem –
Hee has wyth him an Outsyde Broadcast
   teeme.

Acrosse the aisle, two HIPPIES sat
   entwyned,
Hopynge, ere longe, to blowe their tiny
   minde
Upon the Golden Roade to Samarkand,
Then on across the Kush, through Kashmir,
   and
At last drop out in distant Kathmandu,
Where grass is not just greene, but cheeper,
   too.
And there, atte some sleeke Maharishi's
   foote,
They wil spil oute the necessarye loote
To buy such solace as the saint may proffer

Wythinne the termes of Thysse Month's
   Special Offer.
I fynde I greeve for thysse unhappie lotte
Whose yung lyves runne increasingly to
   potte;
Who shal we blayme if, spaced out, zonked,
   they roame,
Seekynge some mysticke cobblers far from
   home?
Since we, all shackled in our bourgeois
   harness,
Can only crie: Yes, we have no Nirvanas!

Behynde these satte another lovynge paire,
Thir fingers loste in one another's haire;
A fond GAY COUPLE, bounde for Old
   Tangier
(A pilgrimage they mayke yeere after yeere).
These worshyppe atte the shryne of Oscar
   Wilde,
And André Gide, thatte othere faerie's
   childe,
Whose fin-de-siècle wand'rings inne the
   soukhs
(So taystefullie recycled inne his bokes)
Soon gayve Moroccan tourism a booste
Still undiminished; for they have produced
(I feere I rayse uponne the reeder's neck a
Hackle) a kind of homosexual Mecca;
Where all the flockyng hordes of gay devoute
May – in the jargonne of thir faythe – come
   oute.
I wysshe them wel: for *chacun à son goût*,
And who am I, or (wyth respeckte) are you
To say that lit'ry pilgryms shal conforme
To sum olde-fashioned arbitrarie norm?
That onlie those who trek to Brontë doors
Shal be allowed enjoymente on the Moors?

Another wyth us wold not see this waye:
He stoode and stared atte them; he was not
   gaye
Inne any sense: al pinstryped stoode he
   there,
And close-cropped, groomed and
   gleemynge, was his hayre.
His firme grippe held a newe attaché-case,

Than longen folk
to goon on pilgrimage

Sharp-edged, with snaplockes (not unlyke
    his face).
A BUSINESSMANNE was he, and that an
    able,
Reared, thoroughbredde, in some goode
    British stable:
Eton, the Guards, perhaps an Ll.B.,
Or else (from Oxenforde) a Greats degree.
At all eventes, a manne wyth Greeke and
    Latyn,
As polished as the leather chayre he satte in
At Knatchbull, Breene & Smythe (Precision
    Tools),
His father's firme. He wold not suffer fooles
Gladlie or otherwyse: a chappe who coulde
Not shoote, hunte, fishe or choose the
    proper woode
Or iron, or thoughte thatte footeball was a
    gayme
Played with a rounde ball, did not fynde his
    name
Among the list of clients at KBS.
Wich may explayne the roten bluddy mess
The companye was inne; and why this
    wighte
Was waytinge for a (cheep excursion) flyte
To Boston, and the Harvarde Bisnesse
    Schoole
In wich this upryte, dapper, sportynge foole

Had been thatte weeke (agaynste his wil)
    enrolled
By al his borde. For they had herde it tolde
Thatte at this founte of holy bisnesse writ
A sowe's eer mighte be processed and made
    fit
To be a purse, and thenne investment cashe
Would beate a path and begge the righte to
    stashe
Itself therein. And KBS wold rise,
A pheenix, to amayze the doubtynge eyes!
It maybe be so: myself, I cannot feel
Much hope of succour to the bisnesse weal;
I saw his luggage: rods, a rydinge hatte,
Four tennys racquettes and a cricket batte.

Not far from him, a small, svelte figure satte,
Be-cloked, carnationed, in an opera hatte;
(He wore his opera hatte one day a weeke,
One day his anti-Russian one, and eek
A thirde, reserved for twittynge Wedgwood
    Benn.)
A MUSIC BUFFE (and Conscience For
    All Men),
Now bounde for Bayreuth and some
    Wagnerfest,
That shryne he worship't above al the reste
(Thrilled by the thought that it was Wagner,
    who

Wold happilie have turned him into glue?)
'Surely you're Bernard Levin, sir!' I cryed;
He turned, he smiled, he hummed awhile,
   he sighed,
And then began a sentence. But, alas!
Hardlie ten minutes were allowed to pass
Bifor they called Flyte BE 151,
And stil his sentence was not half-waye
   done.
(Wich onlie shows how German influence
Wil sometymes lead to compromise with
   sense;
How, with my aircraft throbbynge atte the
   kerbe,
Could I hang onne for Mister Levin's verb?)

Thus, on a suddenne, was I called awaye,
Torne from my felaweship, the straighte,
   the gaye,
The godlie and the mammonite, the freake,
And al the reste I have no tyme to speke
Of. All those goodlie soules, I feere,
   remayne,
Stil earthbounde, meeklie waytinge for thir
   playne.
While you, deere reeder, for thir grippynge
   tales,
Muste needes hange on, and trimme your
   eeger sayles
Until such tyme as they returne once more
To shayre the riches of thir blessèd store.
I have no doubte, though, that thir diff'rent
   tripps
Wil much improve what falls from al thir
   lipps,
Wen, havynge trod thir spiritual paths,
They laye the fruits bifor us: how the baths
In Bethlehem were filthy, how the flies
Were everywhere in Lourdes, and what
   grate lyes
The brochures tolde! And how the bluddy
   guides
Robbed Martha blind! We'll heare it all,
   wyth slides.

2.4.1975

Basil Boothroyd

ONLY FIVE SUMMERS TO WAIT

People go on about airports. Never a word of praise. The main complaint is that you can't tell one from the other: though I suppose that's less a complaint than a slug of conventional small-talk, a change from the weather, the Government and last night's TV.

The sheer hell of getting there is a popular departure lounge topic, introduced with a flourish of original thought and laced with comparative statistics on air and ground speeds. Many a moulded and unswivelable bar-stool have I sat on, over my £1.75 doughnut and mock-coffee, while adjoining strangers give me a breakdown of their day so far. Six hours at the wheel, burst water-main in Mitcham, wife having kittens in case they missed the duty-free, and once they're in the plane it's only ninety minutes to Geneva. Then six hours to their sister-in-law's by Swiss Federal Railways. She has three kiddies, 12, 8 and 5, and another on the way.

It's the tension. You get a lot of this unburdening. A woman in yellow trousers at Kennedy told me she'd been married to three millionaires, all dead, and was worried about her blood-sugar count. These are the times when you hope the request for Mr Trout-beck to report to the information desk will empty the neighbouring bar-stool at the run. This never happens. It's a part of the sameness of airports that no one has ever been seen responding to these appeals.

That, think many, is because no one ever

responds. A man with the terrors of the check-in behind him, his boarding-card between his teeth, his passport thumbed open at its photograph in case they want either or both at the next shuffling queue, he can never remember, and God knows what pocket he made a mental note his ticket was in, is hardly going to dive back into the mob, beating aside small children and yelling, 'Where's the desk? Where's the desk?' passing many a desirable Gents and still vainly searching when his flight is called.

But in fact it happens. Or certainly did at Luqa last summer, when Mrs Boothrake and I were personally paged in a Maltese accent. Still, we were in the middle of an eight-hour delay. Though I had read half of *Kane and Abel*, there was time yet to kill. Besides, who can tell? It might have heralded a bidding to the Executive Lounge. Dreams are free. Also drinks, in those nests of VIPers. We abandoned our two hard-won seats and scotches and found, after many adventures, the tour-operator's clipboard girl. She had missed us, she explained, with a practised click of her ballpoint. She needed to know if we rated our holiday package (a) Excellent, (b) Satisfactory, (c) Poor.

I forget what we said. I know we got back to find ourselves poorer by two seats and two scotches, and had to stand by an open door where we couldn't hear the flight announcements for a fiesta outside with loud fireworks far into the sultry night.

All this is going to change. Anyway, at Stansted.

I've never flown from Stansted. But come the summer of 1991 nobody's going to stop me, least of all distinguished architect Norman Foster, fresh from designing his triumphant £500 million HQ of the Hongkong Bank in, of all places, Hongkong. Next job, under brief from the British Airports Authority, the forthcoming new terminal at Stansted. It is to be landscaped with 250,000 trees and shrubs, a feature long sought by air travellers finally making base in a whirl of anxiety about overweight baggage and whether they left the gas on.

That's by the way, however. Mr Foster has confided, say sources close to Wapping, that his brief is for an 'efficient, cost-effective and joyful building', words falling from the lips of BAA chair- and spokes-man Sir Norman Payne. He adds other words. 'Exciting', and the popular but more difficult to pronounce 'Innovative'. Always a go-ahead lot, the Normans. Mr Norman Foster himself goes further. The new escape hatch will, he says, be 'tranquil, simple to understand, and easy to use. Calm, clarity and convenience,' he continues, 'are the keywords.'

All this may seem a hazy vision, a Canaletto rising from the Essex mists. Not so. The tranquillity, ease, simplicity, calm, convenience and joyfulness, notable lacks at Heathrow, Luqa and Kennedy to name a few, are no figments. The timetable, unlike those at Kennedy, Luqa and Heathrow, is firm. Five years to the predictable opening by ex-Miss Ferguson. Moreover, as if a moreover were needed, the detailed planning application, last week submitted confidently to the Uttlesford District Council, 'is expected to be approved by September.'

That's moving. When you think, I mean, that the Channel Tunnel was first blueprinted in 1802: and not a tree or shrub yet planted for joy at either end of it.

It isn't Uttlesford's fault that I can't find it in any of my atlases. I can't find the way out of Gatwick, an experience shared by many who think their troubles are over when they have proceeded from Gate 91 to the place where their golf bag is the last off the carousel with a No. 5 iron snapped in two. Admittedly, none of my atlases is new. Uttlesford may have been recently rushed up, with pedestrian precincts and a landscaped town hall. We live in quick times. Make no doubt. There it is. Unless it's a *Times* misprint for Colchester. And its Councillors, joyful at the prospect of emptying the neighbourhood jobcentres into a tranquil, and at the same time simple and exciting, innovation, readily accessible, I see, from London's easy and convenient Liverpool Street, aren't going to quibble around with debating points about whether an expected 15,000,000 passengers will be insulated from each other's half-drunken life stories, or the cost-effectiveness of a £2 coffee and doughnut.

Come September, the landscaping starts. Come 1991, innovative tranquillity and joy. This summer, friends, all airports will still be hell.

Hang on. Give it five years. You'll be amazed.

Me too.

18.6.1986

David Taylor

NOTES FOR YOUR COMFORT AND SAFETY DURING ANY UNSCHEDULED SEIZURE OF YOUR FLIGHT

● Under internationally agreed safety procedures, certain listed articles, including live ordnance, flammable or explosive agents, hand-held rocket-launchers, grenades and portable bazookas, should not normally be taken on board the aircraft as part of passengers' personal baggage.

● In the unlikely event of a security malfunction, routine operational difficulties may nevertheless occur as the result of unauthorised deployment of munitions by gun-toting fanatical foreign loonies.

● During the course of any such pantomime, passengers are requested to co-operate fully with the cabin crew and to assist them in getting a grip, especially during any temporary disruption to the sales of duty-free liquors, Peter Stuyvesant and personal requisites which may be ordered by the captain whilst the aircraft is diverted, evacuated, or brought to a complete stop in the ocean.

● During any shoot-out which may occur shortly after take-off, we hope that you will ensure that your seat-belt is securely fastened, that all cigarettes are extinguished, and that any discomfort you may experience is safely stowed in the waterproof bags provided in the seat-pockets.

● In the course of any turbulent phase of the flight, it is important that all passengers remain seated and do not all crowd to use the toilets without first seeking the permission of the officer in charge of the hijacking crew. In the event of any breathing difficulties, oxygen masks will be automatically lowered from above your head but you must avoid any sudden movements when reaching out for air which could occasion crossfire.

● As unobtrusively as possible, you should try to remove shoes, spectacles, dentures and the batteries from any cardiac pacemaker, before attempting to remember how to put on the life-jacket stowed under your seat

● Try to occupy your mind and to ease the tension on board the aircraft, for example by inviting one of the hijackers to tackle the crossword with you or by reading your personal copy of our in-flight magazine where you will find an interesting article by Hammond Innes on how to survive at sea.

● Maintenance of personal fitness is important through any protracted hijack so do try to take a short nap whenever your captors will allow it or practise isometric breathing

and have a packet of our complimentary peanuts. If you find your appetite suffers under the duress, try at least to take in plenty of soft drinks, but do check as to whether these are safe to consume if, for example, your flight has been delayed on a desert strip for more than 7 days. The steward may have sterilising tablets. Certain types of fanatics are sensitive towards the consumption of alcoholic drinks, so do try to ascertain first whether it is wise to try and promote calm by suggesting the crew crack open the last of the duty-free.

● After a period of time, you will be alerted to the end of your ordeal by flashes of light, dense smoke and percussive bangs, during which time it is requested that you remain seated or crouched into a ball beneath your seat. Once the aircraft's chutes are deployed, you should not linger to collect photographic equipment, overcoats or wraps, your boarding pass, or autographs.

● Once clear of the blazing aircraft, please follow direction signs to the transit area where your ticket will be checked and a new boarding pass issued to enable you to continue your journey after clearance through the local duty-free facilities.

20.1.1982

Paul Theroux

LEFT LUGGAGE

Anyone who has barked his shins on a train from Clapham Junction to Victoria – and mine are still growling so badly from a crack I got only yesterday that I find myself seeking relief in Baskerville-sized cans of Pedigree Chum – anyone, as I say, who has bruised his elbows on the 10.41 'Gatwick Flyer', found himself cheek by jowl with a Barbie Doll in a mantilla ('Wouldn't it look super on the television, Reg?') and couldn't see the conductor for the sponge bags and the jugs of Parafino, is sorely familiar with the luggage habits of the English. Five days in Spain and they are as heavily-laden as Lord Amherst on his (1816) Embassy to China.

You might make the mistake of offering them a hand getting one of these bags out of the train, but I did it once and nearly dropped her – Crimplene suit and all – into the gap. The suitcases aren't any lighter than the people, but I've found that if you stoop and wince, muttering, 'I've done me back,' at the same time showing them a tube of Algipan, they wipe that imploring look off their sunburnt faces and heave-ho.

What is it with these people and their ten suitcases? The one-bag braggart is no better – his usually weighs a ton and is so thick with leather belts you suspect him of having taken night-classes in bondage. Most of the returnees have had a short holiday in a hot country, but with their skin the texture of puff pastry and their flesh raw from sunbathing they look like so many immigrant sausage-rolls with all their worldly goods in the aisle. What have they got in there, for God's sake? Boiler nuts? Anthracite? Black and Deckers? Scaffolding? They are dressed like factory workers in Wuhan, so it's certainly not clothes. Is it souvenirs? The carcass of the last bull they saw jinking on to a matador's sword? Is it some shrunken-thighed Dago they're smuggling into Car-shalton for a lifetime of indenture to Hoover their maisonette?

They are, of course, bringing what they think is required. It's interesting. The less people travel, the more they conceive, like the Chinese before them, the world to be filled with hairy-faced baboons who live in utter squalor, or worse, Uttar Pradesh. The first time I went to Africa, people with me – Americans, who boasted of having had a liberal education and who frowned at words such as 'native', never mind 'jigaboo' – brought crates of toilet paper, Kotex, Kleenex. The parting words of the father of a pal of mine at the airport in New York were, 'Got enough flints?'

Flints? I told him that they had probably heard of matches in Nyasaland (for this was where we were headed), as they had recently burned down some civic buildings in their quest for *Ufulu* (Freedom) under the lead-ership of their *Ngwazi* (Conqueror) and *Cirombo* (Great Beast), a tedious midget named Hastings Banda. No, the kid said, the flints were for his lighter. He was going to be in Central Africa for two years and, a pipe-smoker, he had two years' supply of flints for his Zippo.

Luggage is the litmus test that identifies the true traveller from the timid bigot who, in his heart of hearts, doesn't hold with abroad. It is the Awayday Freak and the sunburnt yob on his Lunkenheimer Sunseeker Weekend who is the cart-horse – not the overlander who is headed, carrier bag in hand, for Baluchistan or the Upper Valley of Greater Zap.

We knowledgeable, trustful people travel light. Anything that does not fit under an airplane seat, I refuse to carry. The advantage of First Class – but it is the only advantage – is that you are allowed two bags. Indeed, virtually the only thing the flight staff do in First is serve as left-luggage attendants – but they do it with a smile. As a schlepper in Economy, I have a seat-sized bag, but even if it was bigger than it is, I could find a home for it somewhere among the life-jackets, which are little more than pathetic props for the pre-flight ('In the unlikely event ...') lecture. Planes are becoming more and more like Friday night on the Glasgow Express – cupboards jerking open and spilling tennis rackets on to people's heads, coats and shoe boxes littering the floor, and a valise crammed into every corner.

Mine is under my seat. And my children are in possession of tiny Chinese knapsacks. They hold very little and such is the design of these back-packs that only a child of ten or twelve can get it over his shoulders. Why should I carry my children's junk? And realising that the knapsack is small discourages any belief in their being able to hump Atom-Blasters or Microvision.

I have not checked a bag at an airport for six years. It struck me that by avoiding this headache I had an extra hour prior to travel, and two or more hours at the other end. Who is the first one through Immigration, first in line at Customs, first at the taxi-rank? Need you ask? And my children in Chinese knap-sacks are hard at my heels. I see from my 1980 diary that I spent a total of 168 days outside the United Kingdom last year – four trips to the States, one to Holland, and a month in China: no checking, no ticket-stubs, no watching the conveyor-belt for a burst suitcase that's too heavy to carry anyway, and even if I could, would be full of things I don't need. And when the people are still crowded around the – am I looking for the word carousel? – saying, 'That looks like it ... No, the brown one,' I am barrel-assing down the freeway, already on vacation.

What's in the bag? For China, I took two pairs of trousers (I wore one), two sweaters, two shirts. I wore another shirt, and my jacket. Socks – three pairs; underwear – four. That about wraps it up. Oh, yes, a razor and some blades; my toothbrush. No aspirin (they have headaches in Soochow too). When I think of it I bring Eno's Fruit Salts, but I didn't bring any to China. I wore my camera, my pen and notebook were in my pocket. I bought novels to read – they sell Keith Waterhouse in Canton – but gave them to Chinese hotel clerks when I was finished (what did that fellow make of *The Spoils of Poynton* or Zamyatin's *We*?).

The other people on my China tour were somewhat pitying when they saw my bag, but I had the last laugh when the weather changed and they were saddled with mink coats, steam irons and hair-curling kits that, such was their weight, would certainly have curled mine if I had to carry them from Chungking to Shanghai. Some of these people inquired rather circumspectly about how dirty I got, and what did I do with my dirty clothes? These folks humped laundry bags all over China; but China is a wonderful place for getting things washed. You hand the stuff over in the morning and have it back in the evening.

I did not meet Deng Hiao Ping, but if that had been on the cards, or if I had been scheduled to address the Central Committee or been asked to prosecute the Gang of Four, I would have brought a suit in a garment bag. No need to check it. You bring it on the plane and hang it on one of the many hooks provided.

I am luckier in my visits to the States, since I have a house – and a razor and fruit salts – there, and all the clothes I require. This is a mixed blessing. I still use my underseat bag, but I bring pipe tobacco in it (I have ten pipes in the States, and as I'm not allowed to smoke a pipe on the plane, what's the point of taking one?). Last summer, I brought five cans of Players Navy Cut and the facsimile – ten kilo – volume of Johnson's *Dictionary*. Going through Customs in Boston I was halted by a hag in a uniform.

'Is this all you have?'

The question is familiar: I've been through this routine before.

'That's it,' I said. 'That's about the size of it.'

'Is *this* all you have?'

'I just answered that question,' I barked.

'Don't get smart!'

Smart – this article must prove it? – is something I'm not. But she could not believe that I was spending two months in the United States with Johnson's *Dictionary*, five cans of tobacco and the clothes I was wearing. I tried to explain about the house, but she cut me off.

'Come over here,' she said, and sat me in a cubicle. 'I'd like to know a little bit more about you.' She opened the tobacco cans and leafed through the dictionary and gave me the third degree. I was out of the airport in under an hour – my record is ten minutes from touch-down to taxi-rank – but with a new resolve: next time, I thought, I'll bring a pair of socks.

21.1.1981

'OK, everyone's gone – you can pick it up now.'

Mike Harding

ZORBA THE BUBBLE AND SQUEAK

I first met him in Poros. I wanted to take the boat to Corfu and had gone down to the port. It was almost daybreak, The oily waters of the harbour slapped against the stone piers. Somewhere in the olive groves above, goat bells jangled and a donkey was greeting the morning by choking on a kebab. It was then that I saw him standing huddled and massive by a mound of fishing nets.

'Got a cigarette, boss?' he called as I looked out to sea.

'Life!' he said as I cupped the flame in my hands for him to light his fag. 'I tell you what life is! Life is the goat that eats the old ladies' washing. Life is a drunk monk chasing a chicken over the mountains. Life is a bumble-bee with piles. Life is ... Life is ... take me with you boss!'

I looked at him and shook my head.

'I need peace,' I said. 'I've been working for ten years in a doner kebab and chip shop takeaway in Milton Keynes. Concrete cows, Buddhist monks and Jehovah's Witnesses lost in the car parks. It's been hell! Now I'm coming home to the mountains to write.'

'Write! Write!' He spat fiercely and began dancing in the dust. 'Boss, you're crazy! You'll write words that will gather dust in forgotten rooms. Books that mice will make *souvlaki* from. Don't write, boss! Live, boss, live! Find a woman with breasts like twin moons and a mouth like sunset spilling between the clouds! Get drunk on *raki* every night! Chase the village girls through the streets naked and covered in retsina! Do the Daily Mirroropoulis Bingo! Do anything but write, boss.

'Do you know what happens to writers, boss? They die just like you and me. Homer, Shakespeare, E. Nesbit – dead, boss, every one of them! Lot of good their writing did them, boss. And that Gerasimos Archer, what happened to him? First a writer, now a politician – doubly cursed – from one set of lies to another!'

We disembarked at Agios Sunmedios. The town looked strange somehow. The little cafe of Dimitrios, where once the old men had sat with their worry beads spitting at lizards in the dust, now had a hundred cloth-covered tables spilling across the pave-ment on to the harbour wall. Slim-hipped young waiters were gliding between the tables like black-headed swans and at every table fair-haired, lobster pink people were shouting and drinking and writing postcards.

'I can smell coconuts,' I said.

'It's them, boss,' said Zorba sadly. 'Every year when the hot sirocco has died a little they come and lie on the sand with no clothes on, rubbing oil on their bodies until they smell of coconuts.'

'How strange life is,' I murmured.

'They plug little things in their ears, boss, and there are wires that go from these things to little boxes. Then they press a switch and music comes out of the box into their ears and they sing, boss! All of them sing and hum out of tune! Thousands of them on the beach, boss, humming and groaning like pink walruses in pain through eating too many coconuts!

'And the women, boss – they wear no chest things. And they rub oil on them, boss – just like they're smacking naughty melons! Come with me, boss, I'll show you something.'

We walked along the harbour to the old olive oil shop, now called Athena Art. In the window were a few badly painted ikons, some alabaster statues of discus throwers, a pile of leather sandals and hundreds of brass statues of little boys with corkscrew willies.

Zorba cleared his throat and spat in the dust. 'A boat comes from Taiwan every week with tons of this stuff, boss, and the coconut people buy them. They especially like the corkscrew willie things.'

'Never before have I seen such things,' I muttered – 'not even in Scunthorpe.'

We sat outside a cafe. Some coconut people came and sat close by. Two men wearing shorts and Taiwan sandals carried

bags full of corkscrew willie things; two women with red faces and swollen ankles carried more bags of corkscrew willie things. Across the road at the harbour wall some members of the Greek Society for the Preservation of Birds were rescuing seagulls from a coconut oil slick.

''Ere, my son,' shouted one of the coconut people to a waiter.

'They call us "Bubbles", boss,' said Zorba sadly.

'Bubbles?' I asked.

'Bubble and squeak – Greek. It's one of their jokes, boss.'

Zorba looked sadly at his glass of ouzo.

'They make us dance in a long line with them, then they get drunk and they make us do the thing called Superman, boss. It's terrible, boss. We have to be birds and hitch-hikers and pretend to swim in the thing called Superman, boss. Then they sing the song of the white sausage.'

'The song of the white sausage?'

Zorba nodded. 'Una Palonie Blanca. It's Spanish for one white sausage.'

The tail end of the sirocco blew the smell of coconuts along the harbour.

Zorba's eyes watered as he looked at his drink.

'It's the coconuts that get me, boss. That and the woman from Halifax.'

'The woman from Halifax?' I asked.

'You'll see her tonight, boss,' said Zorba.

As evening covered the island I walked with Zorba to the Square of the Heroes where we sat to drink our first ouzo of the evening outside an old cafe. In the distance a black speck with a baseball cap was approaching, singing a dirty song to a hymn tune.

'It's Ulysses, boss – the mad monk.'

The monk grew closer, his black soutane flapping about his legs, his baseball cap nodding in time to the song he was singing. A snatch of the words sailed through the night air. To the tune of '*Kyrie Eleison*' he was singing:

I'll show you my souvlaki
If you show me your baclava.

He came closer, reeking of sour sweat, incense and coconuts. Zorba dragged him into the shade. He peered at Ulysses excitedly.

'How did you become a monk?' he demanded. 'Was it a vision? Did fear of the Lord drive you into the cloisters? Did you see the devil on the mountains coming for your soul?'

The monk shook his head.

'It was the woman from Halifax,' he groaned, reeling away from Zorba past the garage and on through the dusty olive grove. He belched and the odour of coconuts filled the air as squadrons of bluebottles followed him into the darkness beyond the cafe's lights.

'The woman from Halifax,' whispered Zorba, a nervous tic spreading across his creased old face like an earth tremor under dried mud flats.

It was almost midnight in the Cafe Gerasimos. A table of fair-haired people were shouting and bawling and banging the table.

'Are they fighting?' I asked Zorba.

'No, boss, they're Germans saying hello to each other.'

We sat watching them eating their *souvlaki* and chips, shouting and roaring and banging the table. Then a faint noise in the distance suddenly silenced them all.

A lone voice was singing 'The Birdy Song' in a high falsetto.

With a little bit of this

And a little bit of that
And waggle your bum, oh oh oh oh!
cried the shrill, far-off voice like a screech owl on a weasel's back.

'Ish comen der Frau von Halifax,' muttered one of the Germans as they hurriedly fled the cafe.

The voice grew closer. Zorba, as though he realised that flight was useless, tried to look inconspicuous in the corner. As the noise grew nearer it became obvious that there was not just one person but many and round the corner thronged a gang of 30 or 40 very drunk people, at their head a woman of massive proportions with a turquoise dress and blonde hair piled on her head like a meringue.

'Ey up! It's Zorba! Sithee by eck tha knows,' she squealed, launching herself at him, her bosoms sailing before her like railway engine buffers. She grabbed him by the hand and dragged him to a table. Drunks all round her collapsed into chairs.

'Ey up, waiter cock, sithee!' she shouted at Gerasimos the cafe owner. 'Mucho vino for everyone and mucho music you savvy? This place is like drinking in a piggin' morgue!' Wine and glasses appeared and Gerasimos switched on a cassette player.

The smell of coconuts filled the air. Zorba's eyes watered. From the speakers hidden amongst the wine leaves came the sounds of *bouzouki* and *sanduri* and a voice began singing a beautiful plaintive Macedonian ballad about a poor goatherd who falls in love with a rich landowner's daughter.

'What's this crap?' shouted the woman from Halifax, banging the table. 'Nah then, old cock, get some dance music on you savvy? Mucho danco yes? Musico fasto por favor – old pilloko!'

And as Gerasimos put a tape of Greek village dances on, she dragged everybody up on to the floor. In a corner eleven or so bodies were piled on top of each other, while another group of drunks were being noisily sick in the darkness beyond.

'Yer can't beat 'avin' a good time sithee by eck!' bawled the lady from Halifax, her arm firmly locked round Zorba's shoulders. 'Right everybody, Greek bloody dancing and I want everybody bloody dancing too!' We stood in a long line. Zorba in time to the music took one step forward then one step back. The lady from Halifax did the same. Zorba took two steps to the left then two to the right. The lady from Halifax followed suit. Zorba crossed his legs and flicked the heel of his right foot backwards, slapping it with his left hand as he did so.

The lady from Halifax crossed her legs and fell over. Like a row of dominoes the line tippled to the floor, legs and arms flailing hopelessly. The lady from Halifax got up and made everybody do the Hokey-cokey. More people were sick. Three broke legs and one lost an eye.

Then she made everybody do Knees Up Mother Brown. Two broke legs, one sustained a rupture. After Knees Up Mother Brown she forced everybody to sing 'Ilkley Moor Baht 'at', which went on for nearly two hours because nobody knew the ending. Zorba tried to leave but the woman from Halifax clutched him to her bosom.

'Don't nobody come near 'im,' she shouted. 'Ee's mine sithee by eck! More vino, Zorba! Tonight – you savvy tonight?' Zorba nodded.

'Tonight,' she said, 'you and me's goin to get absolutely rat-arsed – then we're goin to bed, you savvy?' – Zorba nodded – 'and we're goin' to rumpo rumpo till dawn.'

The smell of coconuts filled the air. Zorba's eyes were moist – whether it was tears or water I couldn't tell.

'Boss,' he croaked. 'What's the address of that donor kebab takeaway in Milton Keynes?'

15.1.1986

'Oh, I'd say it's about ten minutes to three.'

'Land ho!'

Holte

AMONG MY SOUVENIRS

'Mind you, it's not what it used to be – even the unspoilt
tribes of New Guinea are out to make a fast buck these days.'

'They're permanently on the look-out for ivory snugg
so how Arthur got this piece out I'll never know.'

'We bought this lovely wallet in one of the back street
Mind you, we had a little difficulty convincing the
Iranian authorities that it was paid for.'

'You press this little button here – and he sings "O Sole Mio"
and makes a grab for your cornetto.'

'Actually they import the mechanism from the Swiss – but the concept is typically Haitian.'

'Norman spent a lot of time down on the quay, watching the fishermen mending their nets. Until one day, they presented him with this lovely jersey.'

'Right, the scene is set ... release the mosquitos, Bernard.'

'For somebody who failed A-level French she doesn't seem to do at all badly!'

'I much preferred it when we were twinned with München Gladbach.'

'It beats me how anyone can scratch a living from tourism stuck way out here.'

Merrily Harpur

AUX ARMES, CITOYENS!

'In this summer's battle for space on the camping grounds of France, the British will find themselves outnumbered 7-to-1 by the French.'

Guardian

'Well, at least there's a corner of a foreign field that is forever England.'

'Fantastic! The fields are just one mass of orange Day-Glo nylon as far as the eye can see....'

'These are dummies! The Johnsons have escaped!'

'This is just like the EEC –
the only thing it's worth
staying in for is to annoy the
French.'

'Only **looks** empty, mate. In fact it's the annual
reunion weekend of the Maquis.'

'What worries me is that by the time we get to the front of
the queue the Morey St Denis 1972 may be past its best.'

'Do you remember,
darlings? We saw it on the
Bayeux tapestry....'

E. S. Turner

TOO MANY COOK'S TOURISTS?

The first Queen Elizabeth did all she could to prevent her subjects from travelling abroad. They were all too likely to pick up wrong ideas about religion, as well as those vices at which foreigners excel.

When the second Queen Elizabeth came to the throne, the struggle to keep the British at home was intensified: that year the travel allowance was cut to £25 in cheques, £5 in notes and £15 for the car, a restriction calculated – as Lord Kinross pointed out in *The Times* – to turn the once Sovereign People into a race of spongers.

Of course, the attempt at confinement failed. Already, in the reign of the new Gloriana, vastly more holidaymakers have left these shores, singly or packaged, than in any previous one. There are multitudes, as the poet said –

    To whom the Cyclades are quite
    Familiar, like the Isle of Wight.
Moreover, millions of these globe-girdling New Elizabethans have never known what it is to be airsick, or for that matter seasick, though a few may have been coachsick on the road to Moscow.

In 1952 a superb, and munificently subsidised, American liner, the *United States*, seized the Blue Riband of the Atlantic. She covered the stretch from the Ambrose Light to Bishop's Rock in three days, ten hours and 40 minutes, a terrific average of 35.59 knots, cutting by ten hours the record held by the *Queen Mary* since 1938. It was the first time

the Americans had won the Blue Riband for a century.

In those days the vast bulk of people still crossed the Atlantic in the great liners, eating up to five meals a day, not counting mid-morning *bouillon* and sandwiches. When the voyage began they wept and threw paper streamers to their friends on the quay. They dressed for dinner even in Tourist, then undressed for bed in the presence of strangers, who might or might not be sober. This was called gracious living. Their reward for tolerating bores at their table for up to seven days was a glorious landfall in the New World, with the cliffs of Manhattan shining in the sunrise. We used to think the *longueurs* well worth it and we enjoyed chatting to such hardy mariners as the ship's gardener.

In 1952 the Viscount was the pride of the air routes. That was also the year when the first Comet went into service, with black consequences. Not until 1958 did the Comet IV and the Boeing 707 begin a regular jet service on the North Atlantic, still with a touchdown in Newfoundland on the westward flight. The ship operators were not too worried, for that year they carried a record number of seaborne passengers on the Atlantic – 1,200,000. How could sea travel possibly fail?

But it did, and very rapidly. Two *Queens* came to ignominious ends and the last voyage of the *France* ended in mutiny. Today one can still eat one's way across the Atlantic, unless the *Queen Elizabeth II* is away somewhere cruising, in which event one may have to go Polish or Russian. One can also, if one has influence, sail in a cargo ship, which tends to be a very up-market experience, with black tie in the evening.

Today's holidaymakers who stream into Europe by car have been spoiled by drive-on ferries, or drive-in aircraft, or extensions of Motorail. Some of us remember when our cars were hoisted up by slings under the wheels and dropped with a thud on deck. In 1952 taking a car abroad still involved an imbecile weight of paper work. There were documents called *Carnets de Passage en Douanes, Triptyques* and *Acquits-à-Caution*. Unless you joined a motoring organisation – and why should you? – you had to deposit hundreds of pounds before leaving as a guarantee to Customs that you would not sell the car, or its engine, on your holiday. Slowly, much too slowly, the bureaucratic follies were abated. Today one can drive straight from London to Bucharest or Helsinki without trouble, or to Moscow not without trouble. Thanks to expanded free motorways one can cross Belgium in an evening and Germany in a day, though in France and Italy the motorways cost money. The motels are dearer than they need be (Oh for those dollar-a-night cabins in America in the 1930s, with almost five dollars to the pound!). For the keen motorist, it's still an agreeable feeling to wake up in the middle of Europe and wonder in which of half a dozen countries to spend the night.

The railway story is a less happy one. Yet a glance at *Cook's International Timetable* shows that gratifyingly long distances can still be traversed in Europe by train, in perhaps less luxury than our forefathers expected. The Orient Express, unfortunately, is a sick joke, a subject for travel writers on the lookout for a gruelling experience. The current timetable says: 'From May 22 1977 it will no longer be possible to travel without change of train from Paris to Istanbul. A change will be necessary at Beograd, München or Venezia ... There will be no sleeping cars in any train between Beograd and Istanbul.' What a downfall for the Madonna of the Sleeping Cars – dozing bolt upright through the Balkans, jumping out at remote halts to buy food! And yet train lovers still brace themselves to do amazing journeys. I know of at least one family who travelled by rail from Kowloon (Hong Kong) to London only a few years ago and enjoyed it. (To our grandfathers such a trip would have seemed less surprising.)

The age of mass travel has been a tale of ever-widening holiday horizons. At first people talked of little but the Costa Brava and the two Rivieras, French and Italian. Then they talked of the other Spanish *costas*, the Algarve, the Greek islands, Rimini and the Yugoslav coast, Tunisia. The French developed the once mosquito-ridden western shores of the Mediterranean. Inaugural flights came thick and fast. Suddenly the Caribbean was within financial range and mass tourism reached Jamaica and St Lucia. If one felt that the polluted Mediterranean had become a dead sea, well, there were clean beaches in East Africa, or even in the Seychelles. If there were queues of climbers – as reports said – on the upper reaches of the Matterhorn, things were a little easier in the High Atlas.

Thomas Cook ran package tours to Paris in 1855, but it was in the present reign that the concept of the all-paid-for group really fructified. Although the operators of scheduled jets had been forced to turn over most of their space to Economy class, the charter firms were out to undercut them still – and if that meant encouraging bogus affinity groups the public saw no moral offence in it. In the free-spending 1960s more and more people were taking two holidays a year, the second of these being, as likely as not, a bold and unabashed bid for winter sun, once the privilege of Cowards and Beaverbrooks. Others went in for astonishingly cheap long weekends in places like Lisbon, Berlin and Istanbul.

Social historians may or may not remark that the age of mass travel coincided with the cult of scruffiness. To the fastidious it was a sad sight to see people in jeans and T-shirts being shuttled in aerial containers from one continent to another, dumped into identical hotels on congested strands, with their dreary luggage and exigent children (the 'child impedance factor' is recognised by statisticians in their analyses of why people do, or do not, travel). To the less jaundiced

*'I think we're lost. This is the same country
we went through an hour ago.'*

observer the sight of a crowded Jumbo disgorging its passengers in tropical heat was a rich and heart-warming one.

People like Sir George Young, author of a worried Pelican called *Tourism: Blessing or Blight?*, feel that something ought to be done to control all this mass travel and to relieve its nuisances and oppressions. He would like to see a World Tourist Authority, but would anybody else? Possibly the most alarming statistic he produces is that 95 per cent of the world's population has never crossed an international frontier. When China and India and Africa at last take to the airways, will the British then stay at home?

6.4.1977

*'This is your captain speaking . . . I apologise for the bumpy ride. We are now flying
at about ten feet . . . Mr Tatlow's had a go . . . who's next?'*

'A gentleman here says he might be interested in the salvage rights, sir.'

Sue Arnold

A MIDSUMMER DAY'S DREAM

Flaming June already and not a holiday brochure in the house. The knife falls from my hands. I forget the *poussin citronné aux fines herbes* I have been preparing for the children's lunch-boxes and I dream. I see a cobbled piazza bordered on three sides by a crumbling, sun-dappled palazzo and on the fourth by a blue, blue lake. I am sitting at a table on the terrace of the Hotel Gorgonzola sipping chilled Frascati. I am wearing white, all white and a wide-brimmed picture hat. Anita Brookner's latest emaciated volume lies open on the table in front of me unheeded, for I am gazing out at the picturesque harbour, with its flotilla of gaily coloured fishing boats bobbing up and down in the water like children's bath toys, where Giuseppe, faithful old Giuseppe, is teaching my small son to mend fishing-nets. On the steps of the quaint mediaeval church of San Altobelli, with its famous frescoes depicting the childhood of Sophia Loren, my daughters laugh together with the local children as they play that popular old peasant game Pass the Pastasciuta and yes, here comes Angela, white Norland cuffs still crisp despite the heat, wheeling baby James into the courtyard ready for lunch.

What shall we do this afternoon? Maybe I shall ask Giulio, marvellous old Giulio, the local ferryman and brother of faithful old Giuseppe, to row me across to the island so that I can take tea with the Contessa again. Although we met only three days ago at the launderette, Contessa Olivetti di Scalopini and I have become firm friends. Her family are descended from the Medici. They have an Abbey in Amalfi, a penthouse off the Villa Borghese and a shoe factory in Turin, but we have a lot in common. 'Ah Suzannah, cara, tell me about life in England,' she says, snipping her thread with silver tapestry scissors that once belonged to a mistress of Lorenzo the Magnificent, 'How I loved my time in England when I was a student at the Loughborough College.'

So I tell her. I describe the extraordinary difference the M25 has made to peripheral traffic going east and the large selection of fresh fish to be found at the new Sainsbury's in Cromwell Road. The shadows lengthen. I can hear my children frolicking harmoniously with the little Scalopini, Bertorelli, Botticelli and Baby Buffo (no doubt they are playing that favourite Italian nursery game Hunt the Osso Bucco) and before we know it, it is time to row back to the mainland for dinner.

I stop dreaming, chuck the *poussin* devoid of *citron* and *fines herbes* into the lunch-boxes with packets of crisps and hurry to Hogg Robinson travel agent to stock up with bedside reading. 'Sorry, we've run out of Blue Sky,' says the girl behind the desk, 'and I'm pretty sure the last Horizon went this

morning. Hang on, I think we've still got some Cosmos. Joyce, have you seen the Cosmos anywhere?' Joyce is persuading a senior citizen, with two Tesco carriers and a red beret, that the Tropical Garden Hotel in Torremolinos would suit her down to the ground. 'The brochures tend to be confusing,' Joyce is saying. 'I know it says only ten minutes' climb from the beach but I happen to know it's a very gentle slope.' 'But what's this about being near a bus-stop that provides regular services into the town?' asks the senior citizen, still holding the Tesco carriers, 'Does that mean we are a long way out?'

'Not really,' says Joyce. She lowers her voice. 'Between you and me, downtown Torremolinos can get a bit noisy what with all that flamenco and bullfighting and such. You're much better off away from it all.'

'What sort of holiday did you have in mind?' says the girl behind the desk. 'Somewhere in Italy,' I say, mindful of faithful old Giuseppe and his nets, 'a small family hotel in a square by a lake perhaps.' Five minutes and fifteen brochures later we have established, Sandra and I, that hotels in piazzas with or without cobbles anywhere within 100 kilometres of any Italian lake are well beyond our means. The same applies to *gîtes* in the Dordogne, villas in the Algarve, self-catering apartments in Majorca.

Even *demi pension* in a picturesque chalet on the high pastures of the Tyrol, which roughly translated means bed, breakfast and Sauerkraut in a field with cowbells, is beyond our means. 'How about one of the big new resort centres in Holland?' wonders Sandra, producing a brochure with what looks like an aerial view of military manoeuvres on Salisbury Plain on the cover. 'The self-catering bungalows are extremely reasonable.' 'No,' I say, 'not Holland.' A friend of mine took his family to one of the new Dutch all-purpose holiday resorts last year. 'How was it?' I asked when he got back looking shell-shocked. 'It was like a concentration camp with ponies,' he said.

Sandra has abandoned the racks full of glossy coloured brochures the size of telephone directories and is now examining a sheaf of flimsy leaflets, many in black and white. 'Have you ever considered camping in Wales?' she says. 'There are some really lovely spots in Pembrokeshire.' The picture on the cover of the leaflet she is reading shows a man with a ginger beard, a red T-shirt, green shorts, yellow socks and sandals frying sausages over a Primus stove. Beside him a woman in an anorak is pegging more yellow socks on to a washing-line strung between two trees. The hood of her anorak is up. Three children in gumboots appear to be torturing a lamb behind a tent. The most unnerving aspect of the whole scene is that everyone is smiling except the lamb. Why is everyone so happy? What's so funny about hanging out socks in an anorak with the hood up? Do sausages taste that much better when cooked by a man with a ginger beard and sandals? All these questions will no doubt be answered by Dai Davis, faithful old Dai Davis the shepherd, as he shows the children how to play that popular Welsh valleys' game, Pin the Tail on the Newborn Lamb. 'Give me all your brochures on camping holidays in Wales,' I tell Sandra.

I shall buy an anorak on my way home.

18.6.1986

Malcolm Bradbury

WHY COME TO SLAKA?

Because it's where it's at this season – put on the international tourist map by a hilarious new travel guide from the author of The History Man *and* Rates of Exchange.

WHY GO TO SLAKA?

Slaka!!!

Where is the heart that does not high upleap at the very merest name of your immemorable city! Slaka!!! city of flours and gipsy musick, of great buildungs and fine arts, we toast you in your own brandy-spiritus!! Slaka!!! great city at the international crossroads, where for centuries people of the most various parts have liked to come together for congress. Slaka!!! bustling metropole of traders and entrepreners, where one time a year exhibitionists of world-wide fame foregather in your great halls of conference in most festivating mood for the justly renowned 'Once-A-Year Commercial Travellers' World Fair'. Slaka!!! sweet city of musicality and song, trios and filharmonias, where each summer the most prodigious musicians of all lands come to perform in amazing fashions at the honoured 'Z. Leblat Musicology Festivi', the highest point of everyone's musical diary. Slaka!!! cosmopolite capital and shop-walker's paradise!!! where in your noble bulevars pricey shops offer at bargainous prices the very best of everythings. Slaka!!! duel of the crown of our favoured country, where the best heritages of old times and the the contemporary charms of socialistical cooperation meld to composite a life-style both antiquated and progressive. Slaka!!! city of allsorts, where in wundrous and orgiastic mixtures the rationalistic clarities of the North meet the boisterous intemperances of the South, the techniks of the West meet the relaxing lethergies of the East, and everyone is delighted! Slaka!!! capital of chic, so when nights descend and the motor-cars swatch on our brightly lightered boulevards, only a short stroll in this fine old town will convince you at a start there is much to be had.

Slaka!!! with your fine sepulchres and your rectorates of baroque acrretion, who cannot smell everywhere your history? Slaka!!! with your laughing boys and your imping girls, who cannot delight in your happy people's?

Slaka!!! with your exotic plates and your nightlife of the chicest kind, who can deny your pleasurabilities? Slaka!!! city which has captivated the soul and bodies of so many of all the ages, who can ever oblivate you?

Slaka!!! Oh, why do I not go there pronto?

MAKING A TOUR IN SLAKA

Slaka: Why To Come?

So much for our backgrounds, but let nothing detter your visit to this beautiful place. Truly Slaka is a country not be missed. Large woods invite sportsmen, and 'vacations in saddel' delight horse-riding fans. Especially lovely is the month of May, when the magnolias bloomb. But other excellent seasons including autum, spring, summer, and winter. However you like to come in Slaka, we oblige. And if our transports or hotels are sometimes not quite perfect (we do not mind to make a criticicm), we recall a wise saying of our Russian brothers: 'A little rigour makes a holiday better!'

Slaka has always been famous to travelers, a land for all of curious tastes. Our own great traveller, Vrop Personip, who stems from Gilt, a town famous for its humours, was asked once 'Why come to Slaka?' He thought for many minutes, then replied: 'Everywhere you go in Slaka there is something, and then a lot more!' If asked what more there was, he thought for minutes, then repiled: 'I do not know, but you will find it!' His wise saw is long-remembered with us. Truly in Slaka travelers have found always that 'lot more'!

So we invite you!!! attend to our cities and townlets, our congress and our festivis!!! We invite you!!! come, rest at our spars and drink the water in our baths!!! We invite you!!! dance at our gispy night-spots, or sip our hot meads and salt almons in our tavernas, or sit under a bird-filled tree and enjoy a village wed!!! We invite you!!! join please our gourmandizings, enjoying our famous speciality 'sarkii banati' (folded pate on a bun) or the great delicatesse of the Pritprip region 'tortosa bakum' (tortoise baked in its shells).

We invite you! drink with us in our vinous regions, and remember in their native sets even the strangest potions aquire a delirious taste! We invite you!!! to our prehistorical deposits, our centres of balneation, our busting marketplaces!!! We invite you! Do you come?

You will not regret. For holiday-making there are fine modern hotels, where your room will often have balcony with WC. For the sun-loafer, there are our fine beeches. For the glutton, Slaka is a lasting festival of oat cuisine. The dionysian disciple cannot fail to be the delicious with our fine local vintages. The hiker will delight in our famous long marches, and the mountain-climer will not forget our faces. Folklore lovers will delight in our yogurt competitions, where dances by pheasants in their long skirts are frequently performed, accompanied by their women on the bagpipes. The archeological digger will enjoy a poke in our many ruins. Theater-lovers will delight in the products of our great 'Gorky-Ensemble' Theatre Company, and do not forget the Puppet Theatre, next to the Russian Embassy, which gives great delight to small audiences. The music-buffer will make by instinct for the great 'Z. Leblat Musiology Festivi', and leave with our filharmonias stil ringing in his ears. If of operatic bent, you will undoubtedly seek out our great 'Oper Z. Leblatim' oper-hus where you may see a major operatic repertoire with the world's leading singers mounted by our great operturge I. Nitove.

Truely, in Slaka there is something for all!!!

SLAKA: WHEN TO COME?

Always famed for its wethers, Slaka offers you delight at all seasons of the year. Springs in Slaka, celebrate in song and story, are a balmy time, when warm zephyrs of the mediterranean meet wafts of the North to create a climat always melba and never extreme. Summer delights us, and when our fine sun brills it is the Slakan way to retire to our lakesidings and make one endless sportfest. Autumn when the sun is gentile is our fruitiest time, when we suck mouth-watered appels and collect the grapes and olives from which we make our exceptionalist wines. Winter with its snows and fogs is ski-time, when we like to slip on our slopes and then make our famous hot baths in the woodshed. Neither hot neither cod, Slaka is through the year long a place of unstinting resort. Come when you like, you find wether to please. When to come in Slaka? Any time!!!

For seasonal coutume we offer this advise. Amost never does it rain in Slaka, but rain-cloths are desirable in some season, mostly spring, summer and autumn. For traditional reasons many of our people carry umbrellas in the streets, so take good care of them!!! In summer bring sporting gears, from the whites of tennis to the latexes of skin-diving. In winter we recommend a furpiece and perhaps it is wise to wear a rubber on your foot.

SLAKA: HOW TO COME?
By airs
The state airline, Comflug, tries to fly to all countries with which Slaka has friendly relations. In a mere 4 hours from London (longer from New York), their weekly flight will whisk you to a new vacation wonderland. The airport at Slaka, 'Flyt'dromo Z. Lebla-tim', is but 5 km/8 mi from the city. Busses to the central Comflug office, Wodji'mutu 217 (no chekkin facilities), depart by the hour. Tickets must be bought in avance at the airport tobacco stall (Littii) and are not available.

By seas
You cannot come by seas to Slaka.

By rails
No direct train-routes like to come from the West of Europe to Slaka. Yet indirect trains from such centres at Riga or Bucharest bring may travelers. Such trains stop at many places, and sometimes at stations, in our country. Train service inside Slaka is of two kinds: quite fast (es'pressii) and quite not so fast (rapidii). There are two classes (III and IV) and IIIrd class is commended to travelers who like their comforts and prefer to be seated. Some es'pressi bear on occasion a dining car, though often reserved for party officials. (Attenzie: photygrafing of trains and transportation systems is a state crime, suspected to severe penalties.)

By roads
No main autoroutes pass through our country, because we like to keep it nice, but British travelers will be accustomed to this. But Slaka lies not remotely from the route Berlin–Calcutta and Moscova–Sevilla. Slakan roads are often asphlat and many are free of boulders. Foreign drivers are permitted an entry at 3 frontiers, Pilaf, Splat and Vitosk. Insurances and permits of travel may be purchased (75 vloskan) from the boarder. There are more than 15 stations of petrol (bin'zinii) in the country, and tourists may buy with western currency at special high prices. Types of petrol: regular (regli), 15 octane, and extra (ex'trii), 18 octane. We practise our driving on the right, but pass only on the inside. Traffic regulations are a little distinctive: e.g. forbidden is to overtake haycart. Also is forbidden to drive at night, drunk, and in a restricted area. Speed limit: town, five vlods an hour, countries, eight vlods an hour. Everywhere there are special police patrols to help you and two you somewhere. Parts of western cars are not availed, but our mechanicals are very resourceful. However you do well to travel with screwdriver and string. Penalties for accident are severe, and our peasants know this and sometimes like to have them. And remember!!! in our country we like to drive with a little excitement, so expect always on the road some surprises!!!

A LIST OF USEFUL SLAKAN WORDS
Some Necessary Nouns

Accident	Venturi	Lift	Up'zippi
Airport	Flyt'dromo	Love affair	Senti'menti
American	Janqui	Maid	Schlaff'rom'froliki
Apartment block	Hi'risi	Map	Plin
Art-gallery	Ort'gal'erri	Milk	Piim
Bank	Bursii	Ministry	Min'stratii
Bar	Barr'ii	Mistake	Pilloki
Bear	His'patchi	Painter	Malori
Bedroom	Schlaff'rom	Parade	Man'fusti
Beer	Olii	Pen	Feduri
Bill	Totti	Petrol station	Bin'zini
Bookshop	Toma'hus	Pipe	Huba
Bottle	Fles	Plane	Flyt'bom
Breakfast	For'tost	Police	Jend'armi
Capitalist lackey	Lackii	Police station	Jend'arm'nosk
	Kapitalistikum	Pop group	Poppi'gruppi
Cathedral	Domo	Porter	Baggi'manni
Cashdesk	Kassa	Power	Potenzi
Cell	Host'rom	President	Cam'radakii
Child	Totsii		Pres'denti
Clock	Tictoc		
Cock-up,		Purpose	Destino
large confusion	Mamor'pilloki	Restricted area	Plaz'scii
Comrade	Cam'radakii		strictico
Confusion	Pilloki	Rifle, gun	Fuseli
Corner	Bendi	Scheme	Zschemi
Country cottage	Dachi	Secret, A	Vedontakal
Curfew	Vespini	Security	Stifufi
Curve	Tvisti	Shirt	Blusi
Credit card	Karti'umperialistiki	Shower	Sprey'sprey
Demonstration	Man'fusti	Stair	Up'ploddi
Dollar shop	Wicwok	State Security	
Drink	Buvi	Police	HOGpo
Duck	Crak'aki	Steering wheel	Versi'versa
Enemy	Mal'volenti	Strip Club	Ort'strippi
Father	Horvot	Subway	Umper'bahn
Foot	Plodi	Tank	Bombom
Friendship	Amicato	Taxi	Tacksi
Greetings	Grussi	Tear-gas	Cri'gasi
Grenade	Gren'adu	Toilet	Evakebo
Head	Krapa	Tram	Truga
High official	Up'rat	Trial	Prozessi
History	Hist'erici	Trousers	Panti
Horse	Hippo	Umbrella	Brolli
Imperialism	Umper'alistiki	Waiter	Garsi
		Wild boar	Lad'slatu

Imprisonment	Con'valeski	Windscreen wiper	Flippi'floppi
Interpreter	Dolmetschi	Witch, wizard	Makku
Jeans	Levii	Woman	Frolikuli
Journalist	Pressi	Woman, married	Frolikuli
Language, speech	Tat'aki	Worker	Prolo
Lie	In'pravdi	Writer	Scriptori

18.6.1986

Alan Coren

THIS YEAR, WHY NOT STICK IN THE SAME OLD RUT?

'Himalayan trekking, European potholing, hang-gliding, aqua-diving, canoe-parties up the Amazon and Sno-cat parties across Alaska ... the trend towards adventure holidays is assuming boom proportions.'

Daily Telegraph

'You'd think after all these years,' said the small man in the safari hat and zebra anorak, 'they'd know where to look for King Solomon's bleeding mines.'

'I'm sorry?' I said, turning my face from the sea and re-steadying my feet against the car-ferry's bucking. 'I didn't quite catch. You know what the wind in the Channel's like.'

'I know what the wind in bleeding Baffin Land's like,' muttered the small man in the safari hat, 'never mind the wossname, Channel. Also the wind in Wadi El Hasoud.'

'You want to try lighting a fag on bloody

Popocatepetl,' cut in a tall man leaning on the rail beyond him, one hand clutching the sombrero to his bitter face. 'Seventeen thousand feet up and dangling from a bloody rope and my old woman hanging on to me left boot and going on about the genuine Aztec chiming clock she bought for her Auntie Fay losing its cuckoo at Camp 3, I'll go mad if I don't have a fag, I thought.'

He left a roomy pause, to enable us to take this in.

'King Solomon's mines!' snorted the small man in the safari hat. 'What a take-on!'

The man in the sombrero glared at him.

'Not only did I fail to light one single sodding match,' he said, 'it took three days before I could get someone to chip the fag off me lip.'

'Don't talk to me about cold!' said a voice low down to my right. We all turned. A short lady in a rubber wet suit, white handbag and petal hat was staring up at us. 'I have just come back from the Wizztours £1,694 Glorious Fortnight Beneath The Polar Ice-Cap. This is not what I promised myself when my poor husband Sydney popped his clogs to the tune of twelve grand compensation on account of catching his head in a trip-hammer up Jas. Furmold Castings Limited, I don't mind saying.'

'A disappointment?' I enquired solicitously.

'You would not chuckle,' she replied. 'Not only was my individual holiday igloo not built when I arrived, but two eskimo workers were actually taking it in turns to widdle into jelly-moulds in order to provide ornamentation for the front gates. It give me no end of a turn.'

'It would,' I sympathised.

'I come back from interring Sydney, and I said to myself: You are not getting no younger, Bertha, you owe it to Sydney's memory to see a bit of the world, else his head has been flattened in vain.'

'You're a wise lady,' I murmured, 'and loyal. But why the Polar ice-cap?'

Bertha sighed.

'I am a bit on the dumpy side,' she said, 'and may not have had my pick of Spanish deckchair attendants. I thought I might have been a bit more to Eskimo taste. I did not fully appreciate about them lowering us on bleeding strings through holes in the ice to examine the sea-cucumber at close range. As I could not get my spectacles on under my face-mask, I could not see nothing down there at all. I used to spend all day in the dark, feeling things bumping into me and thinking about the Grand Hotel, Cliftonville, where they throw in afternoon tea and don't even charge extra for lemon.'

'So the Eskimo food wasn't up to much either, then?'

A shudder rippled the rubber flanks, pitifully.

'Every night,' said Bertha, 'our entire party of sixty-six sat down to a whale. My table, being Number Two, was inside its mouth. I had nothing to eat for fourteen days except head. You cannot half get sick of whale's head, I don't mind informing you.'

'You want to try looking for King Solomon's mines!' yelled the small man in the safari hat impatiently. 'It's all bloody cannibal country. I didn't find out till the fifth day when I went to complain to the courier about the food and found out it was him what had given me indigestion.'

'Lucky you didn't have pygmies to contend with,' said the man in the sombrero. 'Last Easter me and Dolly took one of them Off-Season Long Weekends Crawling Down Inside A Volcano. All the waiters was pygmies. They couldn't bloody carry more than one egg at a time, it used to take five hours to get through breakfast, and if you shouted at 'em, they ran under a stone. We never got near the lava. All we had to show for seven hundred quid was a pumice effigy of King Edward VII, and we hadn't been home ten minutes before his head fell off.'

It was while we were quietly digesting this that a bizarre and heart-rending figure hobbled up and propped itself against a lifeboat stanchion. Encased entirely in plaster, it indicated neither age nor sex, and no more evidence could be gleaned from the echoed flutings that issued from the black hole in the centre of its off-white head.

'Last hang-gliding tour of Tokyo I ever take,' it said.

'Dear God!' I cried. 'You fell?'

'Manner of speaking,' it said. 'Jumped off the roof of the Mitsubishi Corporation, didn't I, intending to See The Ginzah From The Air, Its Girls, Its Magic Byways, as per brochure, got a freak thermal off an air-vent, and went straight through the Sony Building at the eighteenth floor, in one window and out the other. Last thing I remember was eighteen thousand little fingers soldering printed circuits, next thing I knew I was waking up in a crematorium.'

'A what?'

'Crematorium. Turned out they'd all seen me leaping off the Sony Building and started running around screaming *Banzai! Banzai!* Only a bloody cult figure, wasn't I? They picked me up off the pavement and gave me a hero's funeral. It would have been all right if I hadn't woken up on the pyre. They turned very nasty then. Started bloody jumping up and down on me. I only had a sprained ankle before that, now look at me. I'm supposed to be down a pothole in Gwent next Tuesday, they'll have to vaseline the cast.'

'Don't talk to me about potholes!' cried the

small man in the safari hat. 'You're looking at someone who's been four miles under bloody Chad. I was less than three feet down when the canary snuffed it. Couldn't have been the same King Solomon, that's all I can say, unless there was money in bat droppings in them days. Mind you, I got an interesting disease. It's a fungus what gradually eats away your gristle.'

'I caught something off a seal,' said Bertha. 'I go luminous when it rains.'

The man in the sombrero sniffed.

'Two years ago when I come back from a month's trampolining in the Gobi,' he said, 'dogs used to follow me everywhere. Even on the tube. I saw the best people, none of 'em could even make a sensible guess. You could see me any day of the week in Harley Street, walking in front of thirty or forty terriers. It went away after a bit.'

'These things tend to,' said the small man in the safari hat, nodding. 'Soon as I've got me gristle right again, I'm off to the Galapagos Islands. They got turtles there that'll have your leg off as soon as look at you.'

'I've heard,' said Bertha, 'that Thomas Cook are building these big new barrels to hold parties of forty. It won't half cut down the cost of going over Niagara.'

'My wife's brother done that,' said the man in the sombrero. 'He come out two foot shorter. Didn't see much change out of a grand, though.'

'Werl, these days,' murmured the plaster cast, 'what can you expect?'

They all nodded. I looked at them.

'Tell me,' I said, 'do you enjoy it?'

They stared at me for a time. At last, the man in the sombrero turned to the small man in the safari hat.

'You meet some funny people,' he said.

26.1.1977

Thor Heyerdahl talks to David Taylor

PASSING THROUGH

Whether or not the ancient Egyptians primed the pre-Columbian civilisations of Mexico and Peru was not, before Thor Heyerdahl, the sort of anthropological conundrum to keep people tossing in their sleep. (Nor, you might easily imagine, was the puzzle of whether foraging Peruvians had, donkey's years ago, set sail for the Polynesian

islands. Yet the tale of the *Kon-Tiki* voyages has sold upwards of thirty million copies. It financed the trips on *Ra*.) Established opinion on the Egyptians was that they had stayed put where they belonged – along the banks of the Nile, idling their time as accomplished sculptors, pharaohs and mummies. Even supposing, everyone said, that they *had* made a go of fashioning boats, such boats would have been of papyrus. Papyrus is a soft, sappy, stemmy sort of reed. In the dry, it snaps; in the wet, it sinks. Over the Nile, maybe; over the Atlantic, never. The theory just didn't hold water.

The boats didn't either. It was Heyerdahl who was first to see the obvious: that a basket-weave craft drains, even in the heaviest swell. Chunks of papyrus in a tank (the hitherto accepted test of seaworthiness) will sink within days; but then, says Heyerdahl, a chunk of steel will sink still sooner and they built the QE 2 of that. He copied his design from a tomb, assembled an international crew, and a few months later cast off on perhaps the riskiest nautical gamble since the Jumblies. *Ra 1* successfully floated but parted company with its stitching ropes two months out. *Ra 2* was at sea for three months, more or less intact, and reached America. It was possible.

'Yes, I was frightened and no, I am not a good sailor,' said Thor Heyerdahl in London last week as he passed through, en route for Turkey. He's still hard at work on his theories of Asia Minor transatlantic contacts and 'although it is a bit early to publish anything yet, I'm getting some unbelievable material.' (If it turns out that ancient Mesopotamians might well have conquered Samoa in porcelain colanders I, for one, shall not be surprised.) 'I don't have any plans for a further adventure just yet, even though of course it is this which takes the public imagination. They think of me sitting on a raft, they don't think of me in a library or a museum which is where I spend most of my time. I think that perhaps I am a mixture of my two parents – my mother was an intellectual, today she would have been a scientist instead of the wife of my father; he was always seeing his son putting insects on needles and with his nose in big, heavy volumes and he was afraid that I would turn out a cissy. Always I knew that I did not want to be an academic teacher or something. I wanted to do the fieldwork.'

Heyerdahl does not look the swashbuckling Captain Beefheart: he's a sensible Scandinavian, blond, sharp-featured, goes in for woolly ganseys and highly-polished brogues. He was, he admitted, a meticulous, tidy man. He's not rich, despite the successes of *Kon-Tiki*, but has poured everything back into financing his work, solo. 'I am not interested in wealth. I should hate to be poor – that is not what I mean – I want only to be a free man. I'd sooner be a free hobo than tied up as a millionaire.' He's found his freedom in an abandoned medieval village, high up in northern Italy, which he bought and refurbished, Catholic church and all. 'I have the Alps behind and the Mediterranean in front. I begin work at 7.30 and go on uninterrupted until 6. Then perhaps I will strip off and go out into the forest with an axe or on a mule, working so hard until I sweat. Nature to me is my god. If you ask me if I am religious I would say yes. A lot of other people would say I was definitely not. It means only that I don't see my god in a long, white gown with sandals and a beard.'

An accomplished linguist (he can get along in Italian, French, German, English, Spanish and Polynesian as well as his native Norwegian), Heyerdahl is absorbed by man. 'I don't distinguish clearly between men of different races, nor between man today and 5,000 years ago. I do respect Darwin, of course, but I think evolution can be exaggerated as a development in man. In the Galapagos, on Easter Island, talking to Moslems, talking to you: the patterns all to me are similar. Even the astronauts – before I met them I thought they must be supermen.

Now I think that, with training, I wouldn't be afraid to attempt what they did. But I wouldn't be tempted. Our own planet is the one with tremendous interest, I would far sooner, for instance, undertake a mission to the bottom of the oceans. If you want to know what really upsets me, it is the state of the oceans, the pollution that *every day* we observed from *Ra*. We have got to do something about that. And do it quickly. That, apart from aeroplanes, is what frightens me.'

17.1.1973

'It all started one day when the adventure playground was shut . . .'

'**This** is Shangri-la?'

'First of all, son, I suggest you learn to read!'

'And whose stupid idea was it to throw a bucket of water over them?'

*'Frankly, I'd have expected a Manchester-born chap to take to
the Rain Forest a little better.'*

*'What do you mean, let's go South? This **is** South!'*

Alexander Frater

BY BICYCLE DOWN THE OPIUM ROUTE

The fabled Opium Route which winds through the forested hills of northern Burma has changed little since Marco Polo, overtaking an ox on a hump-backed bridge, was involved in one of history's first recorded traffic accidents. The road, poor then, is even worse today, and attempts by successive administrations to carry out improvements have been fiercely resisted by the warlords and bandits whose territory it passes through. The installation of traffic lights several years ago at a spot where subsidence had caused it to fall into a coal mine provoked the heaviest artillery barrage seen in the area since the Japanese Fourth Infantry tried to steal General Slim's Morris Camper. But for the hardy traveller with a keen sense of adventure it offers a unique holiday, and a chance to acquire some unusual souvenirs and one or two wounds as well. Applicants for guided tours should be inoculated against blackwater fever, and carry adequate supplies of blood plasma and snake-bite serum.

The starting point for the journey is the picturesque little town of Komb, reached by the monthly Dornier bomber from Mandalay which, if no executions are in progress, lands on the main square. Rooms are usually available at Murphy's, a British-founded hotel now run by a consortium of heroin smugglers, though guests should avoid the East Wing, which has no roof. Since the waiters are surly and the service poor, it is advisable to take a revolver into dinner. Credit cards should *not* be offered when settling the account. They are unlikely to be returned and, instead, will be stuck in bamboo handles and used as fly swats.

Komb boasts only one travel agent, a Mr Dhat, who may be found in the covered market, behind the melon stall. He is the accredited organiser of tours down the Opium Route and will require a deposit of 1,000 dongs.

There is little to see in Komb, apart from the limestone caves in which dwell swarms of great horned bats, and the visitor need not dally. Mr Dhat will provide each member of the party with a sleeping bag and a Viet Cong surplus bicycle. They are simple, robust machines, and the commodious wire baskets on the handlebars, designed for transporting heat-seeking missiles down the Ho Chi-Minh Trail, will comfortably accommodate your personal effects, including suitcases.

The first leg of the journey winds through fields of nodding crimson poppies, tended by smiling peasants who are so stoned they can hardly stand up, and into the forests where, at dusk, the party will enter the territory of a ferocious, Sorbonne-educated warlord named Sang. A close personal friend of President Giscard d'Estaing, Sang suffers from a severe personal disability – he is a midget – and is widely feared for his eccentric and unpredictable behaviour.

Since accommodation is not available locally, the party will pass the night in a storm drain where, on occasion, Sang goes ratting. Should he turn up suddenly, every courtesy must be extended to him. If he indicates that he wishes to sit on your knee or, possibly, your neck, surprise or irritation should not be shown. Simply help him up and leave him there until he is ready to descend. When he has taken his leave, riding away on the back of a large dog, the party may settle down to sleep – preferably wrapped in tarpaulins to protect them from the giant nocturnal wasps which roam the forest during the hours of darkness. Their stings, while not fatal, will cause a speech impediment which may last for several years.

After a breakfast of nourishing frog broth cooked on a crackling wood fire, the party moves off into a section of the forest which is the home of the remarkable whistling lily. Since they only work when a fresh breeze is blowing, you may have to wait while Mr Dhat makes an offering to the wind god, standing on a rice cake and humming an ancient mantra with a moistened forefinger stuck in the air. For those who are interested in neither botany nor Eastern religious practices, this section of the tour can prove extremely boring, but they may pass the time quite agreeably by waving to the fakirs who live high in the trees, on a diet of nuts, buds and butterflies.

Next day the road passes close to a spectacular ruined temple which is well worth a visit, specially if the custodian can be persuaded to show you the exquisite gilded chair on which Buddha is said to have sat and meditated. The fact that it has castors and an adjustable back should not be commented on as the custodian, who responds instantly and violently to criticism, once worked as a Datsun salesman in Sarawak and his knowledge of English is excellent. Donations should be placed in the old hub cap by the door.

Moving on, the party should reach the hamlet of Fa'ang in time for a lunch of delicious local delicacies. The toadspawn, taken with a sprinkling of nutmeg, is particularly recommended. Afterwards, if the money is right, the villagers will put on a display of tribal dancing in their colourful national costumes of gaily-painted cartridge belts and helmets beaten from bean tins. It is customary to show appreciation of the performance by moaning in unison; under no circumstances should the visitors clap, since this is regarded as a sexually explicit gesture and may result in the offender being carted enthusiastically off into the forest for an exhausting 'ghang bhang' and, possibly, coming out married.

The final stage of the journey takes the party directly through the middle of the world's longest civil war. It has been going on, without pause, for 134 years though, in 1978, the two sides united briefly to ambush a caller from *The Guinness Book of Records* who now lies buried just beyond the first line of trenches. The catering corps of either army will serve travellers with a refreshing mug of *arak* and a pipe of opium, and sell special excursion tickets which, if presented at the Front, entitle the holder to lead a bayonet charge or take part in a major tank battle.

The survivors conclude their holiday of a lifetime at the tiny, silted-up seaport of Bung, where accommodation is reserved for them at the Hotel Kabul, famous for its ancient bath house. There squads of pygmy women wielding loofahs and bunches of twigs are on hand to cleanse and refresh them with a sound spanking. Later, Mr Dhat will say his farewells and vanish back into the jungle, leaving his party several old sheets which, if waved hard enough, may attract the attention of a passing ship.

23.1.1980

*'Of course, some of the sense of wonder and mystery disappears
when you find that it's the local McDonald's.'*

Philip Oakes

THE WAY THE STREETS GO IN CHINA

A short story

There was a long row of footprints drawn in red across the flagstones of Tiananmen Square. Side by side they faced the cameras, their toes pointing to the tomb of Chairman Mao, their heels aligned with the ramparts of the Forbidden City. They reminded John Bridger of diagrams in a book from which he had once tried to learn ballroom dancing. It had been a dismal failure he recalled as he edged into position for the photographer. No one had warned him how difficult it was to marry music and movement.

'Place feet in footprints,' urged the photographer, indicating Bridger's brogues.

'Like this?'

The photographer nodded, the crowd applauded and Bridger bowed. He was becoming used to the routine. Watching visitors face up to the official camera was a traditional Peking entertainment. At the Great Wall he had been pictured astride a dromedary ('The camels is a sort of animals in Inner Mongolia' proclaimed a notice board) and at the Ming Tombs he had posed beside a vase of blue and white plastic flowers. Both times there had been an enthusiastic audience who pointed alternately to him and a display-case within which family groups grinned under glass. The photographs were hand-tinted. Skin, clothing and brickwork all glowed with crude shingles of colour.

'Smile now,' said the photographer.

Bridger glanced from left to right and saw clumps of men, women and children obeying a similar command. He counted a dozen cameras aimed in the same direction, their angles varying, but each of them carefully sited to frame a backdrop of fluted rooftops, the bridge with its lion-topped columns and, high on the terracotta wall, a huge, benign portrait of Mao. Gone but not forgotten, he thought and bared his teeth obediently.

Bridger was in China to buy jade. He was the sales director of a firm which imported costume jewellery and ornaments and it was his first trip to the mainland. He was not seeking quality goods. Novelties International bought in bulk and sold cheaply. But – as Bridger had already informed his principals – it was not junk he was being offered, but bargains. Although prices were keen, profits would be high. He found it difficult to contain his excitement. 'Product top-notch,' he had Telexed London. 'Urge we double estimated purchase.'

Tully, the managing director, would give him an argument. But Tully was still bound to Europe and European merchandise. Cuckoo-clocks hallooed in the hall and kitchen of his house in Peckham and there were raffia-swathed flasks on the dining table. He had been against the Peking visit from the start. 'What in God's name do you know about jade?' he demanded when the project was first discussed.

'A bit,' said Bridger, who had taken the precaution of reading up on the subject. 'It's a translucent mineral and the Chinese have been carving it since around 2000 BC. There are two main types. There's jadeite which gives you the dark green called Imperial jade and there's nephrite – the true jade – which comes in pure white. The Chinese like that best. They call it mutton fat.'

Tully blew his nose loudly. 'I can just see our customers stringing mutton fat round their necks.'

'They couldn't afford to,' said Bridger. 'It's beyond our price range. But there's plenty they could afford.' He opened the sample case which he had collected the day before from the Commercial Attaché. 'Rings,' he said, scattering them on the table. 'Pendants. Necklaces.' He felt like the presenter of some TV quiz, exciting his audience with a glimpse of the prizes to be won. And he had succeeded. The board had auth-

orised his trip. Only Tully had continued to complain.

'A waste of bloody time,' he said. 'They'll rob you blind.'

'I doubt it.'

'They know their business better than you.'

'Then I'll try to learn.'

'That'll be the day,' said Tully. 'Get them to teach you the way the streets go in China.'

'I beg your pardon.'

Tully grinned lewdly. 'Don't kid me. Cuddling up to our Chinese cousins.'

'I don't know what you mean.'

'The anatomical difference,' said Tully, sketching in the air with a fat forefinger. 'Chinese women are different. Don't tell me you've not heard that one. You're not old enough to be let out.'

'No,' said Bridger. 'I hadn't heard. I'm too busy trying to decide whether pigs might fly.' He had deflected the joke, but he had offended Tully. Not that it mattered, he told himself as he pocketed his receipt from the photographer. Tully was a coarse and vengeful man, but he was not in Peking. He could not spoil what was turning out to be a wonderful visit.

'Your photographs will be ready in one week,' said Miss Quo, his interpreter.

'I'll be gone by then. Will they post them to me in London?'

She nodded briskly. 'Of course.'

'Why not have yours taken? As a souvenir.'

'Not today, thank you.' She showed him her wrist-watch. 'You have an appointment in fifteen minutes.'

They were going to a small factory near the Tung Pien Gate to see more jade. Their taxi waited on the far side of the square and as they approached it Miss Quo waved to the driver. He put away the feather duster with which he had been polishing the bonnet and opened the rear door. 'After you,' said Bridger. But Miss Quo stood her ground.

'Please,' she said, waving him ahead of her. 'You are the guest.'

'In England,' said Bridger, 'it is polite to let ladies go first.'

'Not in China,' said Miss Quo.

It was a debate they had been conducting over the past two days and while he knew he could not win it, Bridger was determined to keep the issue alive. He was a correct man and a stubborn one. His wife complained that he was too much of a perfectionist and his two daughers accused him of being stuffy. Most likely they were right, he acknowledged. But he would not change. Correction: he could not change. At thirty-five he resembled his father, a music teacher in Northampton, who had insisted on good manners and clean finger-nails.

Bridger looked like him: tall and fair, with a long, pink face which the wind that morning had parched like newsprint. 'They say it comes straight from the Gobi,' Miss Quo told him when they met on the forecourt of his hotel.

She wore a thin blue tunic and trousers and her lips were stiff with cold. 'Where's your coat?' asked Bridger.

'It is not necessary.'

'But it's freezing.'

She shook her head. 'I'm used to it.'

He had tried to persuade her to wear his sheepskin, scuffed at the elbows and grubby at the neck. But she had refused and he realised that she was embarrassed by his insistence. 'I have my own coat,' she said sharply. 'We all have what we require.'

Driving to the factory Bridger studied her out of the corner of one eye. She was in her early twenties; small and slight with short black hair and almost imperceptible breasts. She had been presented to him – like a guide-dog, he thought – on his first visit to the Ministry. 'Miss Quo speaks excellent English,' he was told. 'She will facilitate your stay.'

He had tried to make a joke of it. 'Will you facilitate lunch?' he asked her.

'As you wish.'

'Will you have lunch with me?'

'No, thank you.'

'Aren't you allowed to?'

'It is not expected.'

He could not believe that she had meant to rebuff him; she was too polite for that. But he felt that he had been set a test. If he could charm her, then his negotiations would succeed. He set about it as if preparing himself for an act of faith.

It was not easy. Miss Quo's duty, as the Ministry made plain, was to escort him to factories and showrooms and translate all questions and answers. She was not concerned with the eventual bargaining: only the Ministry could decide on prices and delivery dates. She was simply a channel of communication; an instrument of use to both sides.

Bridger despaired of ever breaching her neutrality until the morning they saw the best jade. It was no part of the goods earmarked for Novelties International, but on an impulse he asked to see craftsmen at work and without hesitation he was led to the back room where old men sat at a wooden bench grinding the stone into a variety of shapes, feathered like birds and petalled like flowers. Wheels spun. No one spoke. Bridger felt he was being drawn into a meditation. He glanced at Miss Quo and saw her face transfigured.

'Clever work,' he hazarded.

'Beautiful,' she said. 'It is worthy of the stone.' She spread the fingers of her left hand and held it in front of him. 'In China we say that jade has five virtues,' she began. 'There is warmth in its lustre and this is the manner of kindness. Its soft interior may be viewed from outside and this is the manner of rectitude. Its note is tranquil and high and carries far and wide and this is the way of wisdom. It may be broken, but never twisted and this is the manner of bravery. Its sharp edges are not intended for violence and this is the way of purity.' She ticked off her fingers one by one, then lowered her hand. 'We learned this at school,' she said.

'All I learned was how to dodge a whacking,' said Bridger. 'Nothing like as pretty.'

Miss Quo smiled. 'Truth is beauty. An English poet wrote that.'

'Did he really?'

'So we are told.'

It was not much of a breakthrough, thought Bridger as they neared the Tung Pien Gate, but there had been a slight thaw. He flinched as the taxi swerved to avoid a trio of cyclists riding with their arms linked and Miss Quo clicked her tongue.

'Fools and madmen,' said Bridger. 'They're the only ones who survive on these roads.' In four days he had seen six accidents. 'They should be locked up,' he said.

Miss Quo did not reply at once, but turned to peer through the rear window as the cyclists merged with the traffic. 'They care for their machines,' she said finally. 'They are expensive. Six months' wages or more. When they get them they are too happy. They become thoughtless.'

She sounded so disconsolate that Bridger patted her hand. 'Don't worry,' he said. 'It's not your fault.'

At the factory he was shown a family of dragons, their green eyes bulging like beads of caviar. He passed one to Miss Quo as they sipped tea in the Manager's office.

She stroked its scales and tufted ears. 'This is not jade.'

'How do you know?'

Miss Quo scratched the underside of the dragon with a paperclip and pointed to the indentation. 'Too soft,' she said. 'This is made of bowenite. Often it is used to simulate jade. There is no deception. You would have been told.'

'You told me first.'

'They will tell you also.' She leaned forward and whispered in his ear. 'Please be surprised when they do.'

'Why?'

'Because it will please them. They like to give you a surprise. Besides which, I speak without authority.'

That evening she accompanied him to the People's Theatre. The audience smelled of peppermint and wintergreen and many of the women carried small children cocooned in imitation fur suits striped like tiger skin. A compère in a double-breasted brown suit introduced the acts. There was something odd about him, thought Bridger. Moments later he realised what it was. He was the first man he had seen in Peking who wore a collar and tie.

They watched a girl walk the slack wire, two pairs of twins who juggled with plates and Indian clubs, a troupe of acrobats who danced the hornpipe on a hanging rope and a pair of impressionists who imitated birds, locomotives and the roar of a football crowd. 'Are you enjoying it?' asked Miss Quo.

'Very much.'

His boredom was acute but he did not wish to give offence. During the interval he joined the queue in the foyer to buy fizzy orange drinks. 'You're sure it's permitted?' he asked as he handed her the bottle.

She nodded vigorously. 'Small hospitality is allowed.'

'Positive? I don't want to get you into trouble.'

'It's OK,' said Miss Quo.

'OK then,' said Bridger. He blew bubbles in his bottle and put it to one side. 'Tell me your first name.'

She paused, then smoothed back her hair. 'In China last name is first. I am called Lily.'

'May I call you Lily?'

'In private,' she said. 'Familiarity is not encouraged.' She corrected herself. 'It is not the custom.'

After the performance they walked to Bridger's hotel. It was very cold and the dust which had blown through the streets all day lay gummed to the ground by ice. 'Where do you live?' he asked.

'Not far away. In an apartment.'

'By yourself?'

She laughed. 'With five other girls. No one here lives alone.'

'You can't ask me back then.' He raised his hand, anticipating her reply. 'There's no need to tell me. Familiarity is not encouraged.'

'That is correct,' said Miss Quo.

'Do you have a boyfriend?'

'I have a fiancé. He is an engineer, working many miles away. We do not see each other often.'

'I know how it is,' said Bridger. 'I travel a lot myself. My wife hates it. You have that much in common.'

'Perhaps,' said Miss Quo. She did not sound convinced.

As they walked on Bridger discovered more about her. She was twenty-three years old, an only child. Both her parents were dead. Her father had been a cook. Her grandfather had bought and sold jade. 'So that's how you know about it,' said Bridger.

'I suppose so. He died when I was small.'

'Did he have any good pieces?'

'I never saw any. We have no private wealth.'

'Not yet perhaps,' said Bridger. 'But some day . . .' He indicated the billboards flanking the street. Once, as he recalled from television newsreels, they had flamed with the sayings of Chairman Mao. There had been avenues of hoardings lettered in scarlet, urging citizens to be diligent and work harder. Now they bore advertisements for calculators and cosmetics, for Panda detergent and Blue Sky Superior Toothpaste. 'Times change,' he said. He felt an impulse to give Miss Quo a foretaste of the good life to come. As they said goodnight outside his hotel he would have liked to have kissed her. But the hotel porters were watching. He shook her hand and watched her walk back the way they had come. His interest was not sexual, he told himself; it was not even sentimental. He was simply pleased to have made contact. They had arrived at an understanding and he wanted to seal it in some way.

Next morning he returned to the factory where they had seen the finest jade. What he wanted he explained to the manager, phrasebook in hand, was something special. 'A gift,' he said, 'for someone who has been kind to me.' He chose a pendant of white nephrite, the mutton fat he had described to Tully in London, and as he held it in the palm of his hand the manager showed him how the design followed the contours of the stone.

'Flowering peach,' he said. 'Symbol of long life.'

It cost more than Bridger had thought possible, but as he counted out the notes he imagined it lying in the hollow of Miss Quo's throat, absorbing her warmth, reminding her of a distant friend. He gave it to her the next day as they drove to the Ministry. He was signing contracts at noon and flying out that evening. 'Come and see me off,' he said, placing the box in her lap. 'Wear this for the occasion.'

She did not reply immediately and as the taxi braked to avoid a trailer crammed with small black pigs whose snouts poked through a nylon net, the box fell to the floor. 'God preserve us,' said Bridger, retrieving it. 'See what's inside before we all get killed.'

She stared at the brocade lid and slipped the clasp. 'Do you like it?' Bridger demanded.

'Very much.'

'Then try it on.'

'Not here,' said Miss Quo. 'Not now.' She stroked the pendant as if trying to memorise the pattern and then closed the box. 'Thank you,' she said softly.

'Is there something wrong?'

She shook her head. 'It is not your fault. The stone is beautiful.'

'Then what is it?'

She shook her head again, her lips tightly compressed. 'Time for your appointment,' she said. 'Hurry or you will be late.'

She waited while he paid the taxi fare, then walked with him to the Minister's office where they were met by a small delegation.

Through the open doorway Bridger saw a table set with tea-cups and a dish of moon cakes. The courtesies had to be observed, he thought. He turned to tell Miss Quo that he would see her later, but she was already walking away. She held the box in both hands as if it contained liquid and she was afraid of spilling it and although he called after her she did not look back.

Three hours later his business was completed. Bridger arranged the papers in his attaché case and secured the lock. Novelties International had done well. The bargaining had been hard but the deal was good enough to make even Tully's mouth water. He pushed back his chair and warmed up his farewell smile. There would be five minutes of goodbyes, then an official car would drive him to the airport. It was not the full VIP treatment, but the courtesy was enough to demonstrate that he was respected. He peered through the blue folds of cigarette smoke and put out his hand. 'Well, Minister,' he said.

'One moment Mr Bridger.' The Minister motioned to his secretary who set a box which Bridger recognised in the centre of the desk.

'What's that?' he asked.

The Minister looked wistful. 'I'm sure you know already. Miss Quo returns it with thanks.' He raised a warning finger. 'Do not be offended. The acceptance of any gratuity is forbidden. Miss Quo is acting correctly.'

'You don't understand,' said Bridger. 'It was a gift.'

'She cannot accept it.' The Minister took Bridger's hand and held it between both of his own. 'It's nothing personal. But we must be correct. Goodbye, Mr Bridger. Have a safe journey.'

The drive to the airport took over an hour. They left the city and its billboards. The traffic thinned. Lorries gave way to carts drawn by mules and oxen with blunt horns. They passed fish-ponds and orchards in which old women stood sentinel by bonfires

of autumn leaves. There were factories in the fields and, at regular intervals, brickyards in which stacks of corrugated roof-tiles were laid out to dry. The road ahead was perfectly straight, lined on either side by willows behind ditches in which flocks of sheep foraged. At one intersection a policeman stood on a red pill-box, but there was little for him to do. Any vehicle could be seen approaching from miles away.

Bridger opened his case and took out the brocade box. He stared at the flowering peach and wondered how it would have looked on the throat of Miss Quo. After a while he shut the box and watched the road rushing to meet him.

There was no turn-off, no deviation.

It was the way, he realised, that all streets went in China.

17.3.1982

Simon Hoggart

GOING TO THE WALL

A chap I know writes about travel for several newspapers and magazines, so occasionally he is asked by various tourist authorities to give them advice. In the past ten years or so he has helped both the Chinese and the Russians. The Chinese, he said, were tremendously anxious to please.

'No more tractor factories and collective farms,' he suggested.

'Good idea,' they said, striking both off the list.

'No more lectures on Marxist–Leninism while showing people round historic palaces and temples,' he advised.

'Perish the thought,' said his hosts.

'How about a few decent hotels where at

least you can get a hot bath and a proper breakfast?' he asked.

'We shall build them immediately,' replied the Chinese, and that is just what they did.

The Russians, he reported, took an entirely different attitude. Each suggestion would be met with a glum stare, followed by the rubric: 'Ah, but the visitors *must* understand . . .'

The Chinese are terrifically keen to give satisfaction and to have you tell your friends you've had a spiffing trip. Things do go badly wrong on occasion, but then the anguished apologies almost make it worthwhile. If you make a suggestion, so much the better – it is another insight for them into the baffling ways of the occidental mind.

So, in the politest possible way, it is necessary to nag your guide. Say, for example, that the prospect of another evening watching chaps in traditional lion costumes jiggling across a stage to the sound of very small cymbals fills you with a drear foreboding. Simply announce, as we did, that you would prefer to spend the evening wandering around the night markets of Peking. Your guide will probably beam with pleasure, delighted that she (or possibly he) has avoided the embarrassment of taking you somewhere you don't want to go.

If you're fed up with the food (one of the most obvious facts about China, yet it still comes as a surprise, is that Chinese people eat Chinese food three times a day), then you can ask to go to a different restaurant. In Shanghai we requested a 'crab feast', a meal several hours long consisting of crab cooked in a dozen different ways, culminating in a pile of steamed crabs. It cost a few pounds extra, but then it would cost far more here, if you could find it, which you can't.

Of course the sights which are on every tourist itinerary are marvellous and, as the French say, each does *vaut le voyage*. They are also very crowded. In the Summer Palace on the outskirts of Peking, reached by the

Chinese equivalent of the North Circular Road – one of the most depressing thoroughfares I have ever seen – it was hard to move. The scores of splendid buildings have equally splendid names: 'The Pavilion for Listening to the Orioles', for example. Near The Hall for Dispelling Clouds, I heard a guide who had some difficulty with her English pronunciation explain to an American: 'Here is Hall for Despairing Crowds.'

'Oh yes, I can see why,' said the American, sympathetically.

At the Great Wall the crowds were so thick that you had to queue to get through the watchtowers. Most of the visitors are Chinese, who are nowadays able to travel more easily, and are discovering their own country in a daze of delighted wonderment. Almost all of them carry cheap twin-lens reflex cameras, made in China, of the type which were popular here around the war. They photograph each other in their thin cotton costumes against each famous spectacle, with all the passionate precision of Westerners or Japanese.

But the crush cannot spoil the Wall, which marches majestically over the mountain ridges, just as it does on the tea-towels. Incidentally, the belief that the Wall is the only man-made object which can be seen from the Moon is obviously absurd. There are parts of the Wall you can't see from the Wall.

But, as seems to happen frequently in China, the best moments are the unscheduled ones. At the end of the mile or so open to tourists, I climbed unchallenged over a barrier and strolled along a part of the Wall which hasn't yet been restored.

After a while I came upon a couple of workmen eating their lunch. They insisted in sign language that I shared it. So we sat beaming at each other as we chewed hard-boiled eggs and cold duck and swigged a rice spirit I had mistaken for beer and which left one hemisphere of my brain detached from the other for several hours. But through the haze in my head and on the hills I could see the Wall striding over the peaks, climbing, dipping and turning back on itself, looking almost exactly as it must have done four hundred years ago.

There are aggravations too. Expecting a leisurely and even luxurious cruise down the Yangtse, we were told at the last moment that our second-class cabins had been taken over by 'big potatoes', agreeably quaint English slang which turned out to mean, disagreeably, senior Communist Party officials. So we spent three days in third class, eight to a cabin, with metal floors, no curtains, and two loos for 72 bottoms. Even here, though, there was one touch of the promised luxury. A steward came in each morning to change the spittoon.

Yet it's curious how you don't, in the end, mind. We relieved our trifling adversity by drinking too much and playing extremely silly games in our cabin. During one of these a big potato came and stared in through the door, his expression both rapt and blank, unable to comprehend the wonders before him.

Two days later we were in Shanghai and again it was a departure from the tour which made the visit memorable. The Peace Hotel on the waterfront was built in the 1930s, and its band of elderly musicians somehow survived the Cultural Revolution with membership and repertoire intact. In the ballroom, the tourists drank forgotten pre-war cocktails and a few danced slowly to *Blue Moon* and *Misty*.

We followed a sign upstairs to the Billiards Room where an old man, far older than the hotel, brought us beer. As we played he sat smiling, nodding and maybe half-asleep. Now and again he would murmur, 'Good shot' through the gloom, more to himself than to us, perhaps vaguely remembering the days when the hotel was thronged not with tourists, but with merchants, officers, ticket-of-leave men, lascars and prostitutes – a despairing crowd, if ever he saw one.

16.1.1985

Clement Freud

A NIGHT ON THE TILES

'By the end of the fifth course I agreed that a kneeling Japanese waitress represents a more acceptable form of grovel than you get from unctuous English head-waiters.'

Since I last wrote at you, I have been to Japan. I went to address Japanese politicians via Japanese interpreters and I do not know, may never know, whether what I said got across to those who came to listen. When you land a British or American interpreter, you know that at least one other person understands what you are saying. With a Japanese – who sometimes takes one short sentence from you and gives it twenty seconds of his verbiage – you have grave doubts; to ask for clarification entails loss of face, and Japanese don't go in for that much.

On reflection, *how* did Mr Watimobo translate my contention that such and such a move would give a man the power of judge and jury? On the day following that meeting, I learned that there is no jury system in the land of the rising son.

I went from meeting to meeting, most of them held in the inner offices of Members of the Diet and House of Representatives. In the outer offices they bundle visiting-cards into sacks and prepare refreshments. In the sanctum they talk and take photographs and become recipients of the appropriate food and drink.

At one particularly up-market meeting, a lady with a hair-brush arrived and combed the Ministers' hair just before the official photographer came to take the duty picture. At another, I was sandwiched between the

US trade delegation and the UK Ambassador, and received the full treatment: green tea, and a plate containing a jelloid grey substance that lurked on the plate and doubled for sugar; immensely heavy pastries that were truffle-like in consistency, glazed with a shiny icing and imbued with essence of Brut such as Henry Cooper used to recommend; then strawberries, their bases cut so that the peaks pointed evenly to the ceiling, and finally cups of coffee.

What is interesting, different anyway, is that in Japan there is no element of 'Please eat and drink – you will find it delicious.' It is quite simply 'We know who you are and have taken great trouble to manifest the extent to which we value your presence here.' Japanese courtesy is overwhelming; it makes one feel very inadequate and the fact that they laugh when they do not understand actually compounds the fundamental difference between our two nations.

They had arranged a television interview for me: $10\frac{1}{2}$ minutes on a morning talk-show. I said, 'If it will help the cause, of course I will appear, but how will it further freedom of information?' They laughed (I later found out that they laughed because all politicians need to appear on TV and for one to question this is ludicrous) but I insisted that I be given a reason and they laughed more and more. So I gave up and went on this show, where I cooked a Reform lamb cutlet and a soufflé omelette and said, 'Were it not for the freedom of information movement I would not be here,' but the interpreter did not pick that up.

When it was all over, the TV people and my minders said, 'Thank you,' and, 'It was ruvly.'

I said, 'But *why* did I do this?' They all laughed again.

On my last day I lunched with a Member of the upper house at a famous Tokyo restaurant where the staff met us at the door of our private room, kneeling and bowing as we entered. We sat on the floor, and had a waitress kneeling beside each of us, filling our glasses with saké, and helping to serve our food. I said to this man (who had been to Oxford), 'How does the kneeling and bowing go with your known left of centre, egalitarian politics?'

He told me I had missed the point. These were waiters, pursuing an honourable profession with skill and dedication. If he invited the woman to go out with him, they would talk as equals – and the waitress nodded eagerly. By the end of the fifth course I agreed that a nice, skilful, kneeling Japanese waitress represents a more acceptable form of grovel than you get from unctuous English head-waiters.

I had a number of meals in Tokyo, some ruinously expensive (my hotel charged £6 for a portion of rice to go with a £16 stuffed quail) and others fun and good value. For about a fiver each in a downtown bar we had a four-course meal with wine, the food served on glazed flat tiles which made it stunningly attractive. There was an aubergine grilled with oil and ginger, glistening from its tile like a leech on a linen sheet. Then a pair of baked potato-halves strewn with spring-onion tops. Then steamed scallops on a tile which was a Queen Mother shade of green.

'Did you enjoy the food?' asked my hosts. 'Yes, and I loved the tiles,' I replied. 'Can I buy some to take back home?'

The restaurant manager was summoned and said that the tiles cost about £1.50 each and if only he had bought more, I could have bought some from him, but alas . . . We went to a shop that sold glazed dinner tiles; the cheapest, which were smaller and fussier than those I wanted, cost £8 each

I shall ask my local pottery to produce a set for me but they are not for all occasions and may not be compatible with knives and forks. Perhaps when the interpreter next comes to England to brush up on his linguistics . . .?

4.3.1987

'– off, Rommel!'

'Sounds adventurous. I read all the brochures but these diseases are new to me.'

THE WIGAN–NEPAL TRAIL

As Sam Hinchcliffe prepares for the adventure holiday of a lifetime, faithful chronicler BILL TIDY reports

'Sorry, mate, but it's a bit too late to tell us you haven't got a baby!'

'...ink of it, luv. In a few weeks you could be plastering mud from the Ganges on your face.'

'What are **you** worrying for? They went last year and **she** was made a Virgin of the Sun God!'

'That's all right, luv. Your family's more than welcome to our seat.'

Basil Boothroyd

HIGH, WIDE, AND HANDSOME

A London clubman in one of Anthony Powell's early books feels obliged to excuse the cut of his dress suit: 'I bought it in Athens before the war.' This was the first war, of course. But I was reading it before the second, and the line stuck in my head as a sizzlingly sophisticated throwaway. Not the dress suit. Never mind that. I'd got one of those myself around that time, for the Farmers' Ball, Horncastle, Lincs, and any excuse I may have offered for its cut would just have been about misunderstandings over the postal measurement form. Well, I suppose I might have said that I'd had it made in London, which would have been impressive enough in terms of romantic places ... But Athens! It was as remote from visitable reality as Ursa Major. (I was going to say the moon: you have to keep updating your idiom these days.)

Well. By the time you read this I shall have been in Athens last Wednesday, if that isn't too confusing. Three and a half hours from London's umbrellas, and the sun comes whanging off the Parthenon and associated buildings like a flaming arrow. From the babel of Heathrow's loudspeakers to the sprawling buzz of the basking drinkers in Syntagma Square ... and trying to believe, for one's conscience's sake, that those damned Colonels are really throwing their shadow over it all.

What? Well, yes, there's the money. But I don't suppose the dress-suit man went for nothing. It was also less convenient. Let's see now – a hansom from the club to Victoria, unload bags, count them on to the Dover train, fight for porters, choppy old crossing to Calais, fight again; Paris, change trains, hang around; Basle, I suppose: Trieste, Zagreb or somewhere – I don't know, I've never done it, and never shall now – Sarajevo, a dump without even a niche in history at this time, and sounds just the place to lose the luggage and find you're on a stopping train to Sofia by mistake. An anxious business, and long. Poor upholstery, no free meals, no hostesses in cute hats, or confident messages handed back from the chef du train saying you're just passing over the Jungfrau and you've only an hour or so to go. Your pre-1914 dress-suit man, if he only had a fortnight's leave to do his romantic foreign shopping, would have to be in and out of his Kolokotroni Street tailor's pretty smartly if he didn't want to miss the train back. Cost? No idea. But I'll bet his hairdresser couldn't manage it. My hairdresser's jetting to Venice this year, and my wife's, for reasons best known, to Budapest. Oh, yes, since the Wright Brothers first got off the ground, through a long line of improvements right up to Frank Whittle, you can be seven days away from the office and still spend six and a half of them in Malaga, trying to forget the boss. The only risk is that he may be there too – though possibly not under the terms of your cut-price package deal, which seems to work out, by some inscrutable mystery of accountancy, about the same as a quick burst round the Lake District.

Who wants speed? The question is put. I've put it before now. How can rushing about the sky at six hundred miles an hour, they say, compare with the murmurous rhythm of the train wheels, the exciting glimpses of Dijon station at midnight, with actual French railwaymen rolling genuine French milk-churns? It's a matter of opinion, naturally. What most appeals to you about Rimini, Estoril, Corfu – being there or getting there? Only an idiot, surely, would say ... But you've a right to your opinion. Mine is that if you're so long getting to

Naples that you haven't time for a sniff round Pompeii you might as well save your money and wait for a good travelogue to hit your local Odeon.

An unnaturally rapid change of scene, they say, is upsetting to the system. Unnatural, too. Perhaps so, for people who've lost their childhood appetite for spells. The magic carpet and the seven-league boots seemed so delicious; it was part of life's great disillusionment to grow up and find they never lifted off the pages of the book. But here they are, and it's the unnaturalness that's half the fun. Don't tell me the stagnant spirit isn't refreshed by a neat trick like breakfast in Belsize Park and tea in Toronto (not that I've ever had either, but you must get your alliteration where you can). Even on the smallest scale I respond: even to the bit of piston-engine wand-waving that hops me in twenty minutes from Lydd to Le Touquet – suddenly, in the time it takes to write a postcard saying you're off all right, here are all these new people, wearing berets and yesterday's shave and talking in a strange tongue. Beat that, Merlin.

Although it's passed through a lot of comics and disc-jockeys since then, that was originally a *Punch* joke about the caterpillar saying to the butterfly, 'You'll never get me up in one of those things.' Poor, deluded caterpillar, thinking it could avoid the inevitable. We all fly eventually. The interviewed centenarian can't stagger the readers any more with that old gag about never having been in a train or seen the sea. It's never having flown or seen the Mediterranean (at the least) that astounds us these days. My wife came the caterpillar line for years. I blamed it on the wealth of old telefilms that keep trying to wring another squawk out of the plot that has the pilot and co-pilot unconscious from an obscure virus, and a hundred passengers being talked down by ground control, with a man at the instrument panel who doesn't know his air-speed indicator from an eight-day alarm clock, not to

mention fog closing in down below and a time-bomb hidden in the baggage compartment. (They're still running these films, I notice, mostly in our last fortnight before take-off.) I don't know what it was that got her up there in the end. Possibly a wealth of old telefilms about the *Titanic*, timed to coincide with our riffle through the cruise brochures. But she gave up struggling around at sea-level in the end, unstuck her countless little aching feet, sprouted wings, and began flitting from tarmac to tarmac with the abandonment of a Rod Laver.

But with less frequency, of course, which is the secret of success. If all airports look the same, how much truer of all tennis-courts? Commuting between Wimbledon, Forest Hills, Paris, Mexico City, Buenos Aires, and nothing to choose between them but the umpire's accent – this must certainly wipe a lot of the wizardry off it: though Laver and Co. may not mind missing the magic; they reap a few material advantages. Much as we love them, when they deign to drop out of their giddy circuit on to our own patch from time to time, they'd soon find us losing interest if they didn't scoop up their rackets and prize money and jet off elsewhere for a bit. Theirs is a short earning life. As long as you can manage Los Angeles today and Bournemouth tomorrow you can keep up the optimum take. Uneconomical loitering around by train, boat and bus could make the thing hardly worth going in for.

Airborne statesmen, on the other hand, probably don't feel even this much affection for the ten-miles-a-minute world, and could make out a better anti-Whittle case than anyone. Harold Wilson can whizz from Whitehall to the White House without bettering his £14,000 p.a. by a bob, and must look back wistfully to the restful times of Gladstone and Disraeli. If they ever went anywhere, and I don't know that they did, they had six or seven quiet weeks in transit to get their notes together. Five hours, and not knowing whether your stomach's lunched twice or not, adds a pressure to life that you didn't bargain for when you climbed the Huyton hustings twenty years back.

Still, never mind the tennis players and politicians. Don't even worry about the high-speed boredom of David Frost. They're overdoing it, and it's not the jet turbine's fault. For you and me, twice a year maximum into the wild blue yonder, it's great. Beats your stage-coach and mule any time. Agreed?

See you in Venice, perhaps ... Algiers, Garda, Taormina, Nairobi ... Even Athens. But you'll have to hurry to catch me there. That was last week.

11.6.1969

'This is the smoking section, sir. Non-smoking is confined to designated areas, including the aisles and lavatories.'

'Why not admit it, Henry – you don't like people to notice you're scared.'

'And I'd like to add that the hijackers were very considerate – much
more than the regular crew earlier in the flight – about enforcing
no-smoking regulations!'

'Look, if you don't want to watch the movie you can sleep. But we can't have you reading.'

'They all dashed out before the National Anthem.'

*'And keep your eye on this little light at all times. If it blinks
out it means the airline has gone bankrupt.'*

*'Just because we are English you needn't think my sister and I
won't make a fuss about this.'*

Sally Vincent

TIME OFF FOR STRANGE BEHAVIOUR

Last summer I motored across Europe to the tip of Greece's index finger. This year I'm changing the chairs round in the sitting-room because I now know that it's the only kind of refreshment I can take. I should have known I was delicate. When I was very young and they were called reefers I smoked a whole one and nearly died of laughing. I can still recall the pain of a totally exhausted solar plexus heaving away as the light went, but to this day I am convinced there is something intrinsically funny about the sight of somebody threading a spring onion through a hole in a piece of cheese and eating it. In other words, if you muck around with perception, something sticks.

I find the psychology of the holiday similarly freaking. For the other lumpenprole eleven months of our annual existence we carry in our heads a model of the world we inhabit, a kind of convenient *idée fixe* of home, work and the shape of things in general which prevents us making little social gaffes like cleaning our teeth in the supermarket or taking a football rattle to the opera. Our little 3D map comprises habit, familiarity and normality.

It allows us to find the keyhole in the dark, to score the hatpeg nine times out of ten, to toe the cat's bum with just the right degree of violence as it escapes through the catflap, and to compose an early morning cup of tea with an efficiency that quite belies our state of malingering undeadness. Then we holiday. Brutishly we cut ourselves off from all familiar territory and go blundering into the unknown in the forlorn hope that bougainvillaea smells better than the roses we've already got up our noses but have long since forgotten to notice. And we wonder why we flip our lids.

My old granny had her way of dealing with the problem. On her first twenty summer holidays spent in Bognor Regis she used to take all the family photographs and place them on the boarding house mantelpiece. Then, so accustomed did she grow to Bognor Regis, she didn't bother to take them for the next twenty years. Well, good for her, but I'm not one of those people who paper their caravans with the same stuff they've got up in their living-rooms and I like to think that owning a passport makes me a more cosmopolitan lady than granny was. But then I like to think a lot of things. The truth is that I was probably clinically psychotic by the time we hit Dover. Maybe you'd call it travel nerves. I wouldn't.

Look. I've got tickets, travellers' cheques, passports, visas, everything in this more than adequate real leather folder inside this still more than adequate tote-bag. Right. Sit in car. Check tote-bag for folder and check folder for tickets, travellers' cheques, passports and etcetera. Shut car door. Lock car door. Fasten safety belt. Off we jolly well go then.

Now riddle me this. Why do I have to keep on checking that they're there? Do I imagine that somebody might creep up the air vent and steal them while my back's turned? What is this unbearable tension that can be alleviated only by opening up the tote-bag for the nineteenth time and scrabbling about inside?

Then, when I get to a terminal of any kind, why do I have this compulsion to crowd anybody in a uniform with a peaked cap on top of it like they were the fountain of life? Please am I in the please right place please at the please right time please sir – to a postman. I know a lot of perfectly sane people are uneasy about missing things, but why should I need a peaked cap to read something off an indicator board specially for me? Why am I always too far gone to believe a loud-speaker?

Common-place symptoms of anxiety, you say. But that doesn't account for the ghastly and overwhelming attack of agoraphobia I had up an Alp. I have no fear of heights. As a child I dove head-first off the highest board in Chelsea baths and I couldn't even swim. But by Switzerland my sense of placelessness reached such a pitch I went stone cold and kept making embarrassingly involuntary gibbering noises. Confronted by anything resembling a view I had to keep my eyeballs glued to a piece of shirting in the vicinity of the driver's left shoulder because it seemed like the only toe-hold on life I had left. And the further I got from home the closer catastrophic expectation crept to catastrophic certainty. Of two thousand cars disembarking into Greece, mine was going to be the one to stall on the vertical ramp. Of a mere fifty on the ferry over about a hundred yards of Ionian Sea, mine was going to be the one to have its wing mirror caught in the lift gate and dragged into the water. And I'm stiff with it.

I can still remember standing there, looking into the sea and weeping, actually weeping with desolation for a beer can somebody had callously thrown overboard. I couldn't move my leg. I'd got hold of some bit of gangplank bar, presumably placed there for the purpose of being held on to, and I thought, Christ, this is It. This Bar Is Dirty. WHAT THE HELL AM I GOING TO DO. I'm stuck here for ever. If I move my hand I'll have to shift my weight onto the other foot and I'll drop my hand AND GET MY TROUSERS DIRTY. Paralysis. To say the moment passed is only a rationalisation of what happened next. I mean, I'm not still standing there.

And the misery has only just started. I keep hearing this terribly loud, terribly

English voice coming from about an inch under my nose. I'm tooting up anything with a GB plate, waving hysterical hellos to people I wouldn't pass the time of day with at home, only now we're all exiled in hell, huddling together at petrol stations exchanging idiot facts to console, succour, heal and identify each other in our hour of desperation. No wonder the louts and touts who hang around all the big motorway filling stations are so successful. 'Excuse please I theenk you Engleesh,' they open with, and 'yes, YES,' you cry, giving yet another gold-toothed Italian superspiv his first psychological lever, an eager affirmative. You're so pitifully grateful to be recognised as belonging somewhere, as having a real home somewhere away from this vast lostness, you buy his ill-gotten rubbish just to keep the transaction going.

There's no comfort in knowing everybody's as mad as you are. Take the tourist at Mycenae – out of it, poor buggers, by 4,000 years in terms of emotional territory as well as several thousand miles – and they're *barking*. There are all these little groups of them, not just reading aloud, but bellowing aloud from their guide books with the insistent rhythm of a motherless child chanting a song over and over to itself, rock-rock, rock-rock, until such times as its comfort is restored. ME. ME. ME. Watching the German didn't help much, either. I watched the maniac for two weeks and every morning he dragged five gigantic gas cylinders from outside a tiny shop and down a back lane so as to secure for himself a piece of ground he had designated, for reasons best known to his lost heart in this totally isolated spot, as His Parking Space. The task would have snapped Samson's spine, but this old guy did it, religiously, every time he moved his motor. He just had to have it.

I get my bit of space by a less dangerous ruse. I never quite unpack. My suitcase, that is. No, I always leave a bit in the bottom so that I know always that somewhere in whatever foreign clime there are these woolly knee socks and these four bikini tops that will remain forever England.

A lot of people, I find, are driven to kill out of homesickness. On just one morning on one laughably idyllic beach I watched a perfectly ordinary looking woman lay three scarlet starfish out on a rock and then devote herself to straightening their tortured limbs as they curled in their death throes. She was smiling to herself. And next in line to her a jolly French family with a kind Daddy who had caught a huge crab so as to amuse his children. They had it trapped in an empty bucket. Whenever the poor beast managed to upset its prison and make a scurry for the sea, they'd all laugh to watch Daddy reclaim it and pop it back so as not to disappoint the kiddies in their need to watch Mr Crab suffer. When you're all washed up on the sea-shore and many miles from home, you've got to keep your self-respect, right? Be seen to be in control? Right?

I think that was about when I took myself into the sea to snorkel my way into obliviousness of the whole stinking human condition. And lo! the beauty of the deep, the darling fishes sparkling and dipping in their wondrous fishy way. And out of the dark and into the light comes a walloping great man, black racing flippers, oxygen mask, dagger strapped to his calf, axe in one hand and harpoon gun in the other, searching, circling, searching, circling, desperate for something to kill. You can't get closer to the illusion of self-control than when you're actually engaged in doing a murder.

I saw the demented swine sitting outside a cafe later that day, writing postcards to his loved-ones in Stuttgart. For all I know he was writing words very much after the effect of my own. 'Wish you were here,' stuff like that. Did he know, I wonder, deep down in his murderous soul that what he really-truly-honestly meant to say was 'Wish I was there. Wish to God I wasn't here.'

24.1.1979

'*We asked the travel-agent to suggest somewhere with quiet beaches.*'

'Bloody hell, Jeanette, I thought **you'd** cancelled the Jehovah's Witnesses.'

'He's a glutton for work – that's as close as he ever gets to a holiday.'

'Bit of luck, that – landing a cushy summer job.'

'Look, if it upsets you so much, Harry ...'

Michael Heath

HOLIDAY ROMANCES

'I've spent my life looking after a selfish old mother, working in the same office ... this is my first holiday and it's cost me all my savings – you **have** to break my heart!'

'We could go back to England, we could get married, I could, how you say, sign on.'

'Try not to get carried away, Miss Greenblat – I assure you that back home I'm just an ordinary guy.'

'Of course I'd love to get married, darling, but you see, I can't sustain a relationship if I know it's not going to end.'

'Darling, I think our affair is over.'

Larry

HOTEL
MIRAMAR

(unfinished)

'There is a notice in each compartment which clearly states:
"Do not lean out of the window in the tunnel" . . . !'

PONT: *THE BRITISH CHARACTER. Love of Travelling Alone*
(1937)
Reproduced Jan. 8 1969

Alan Brien

ON THE WAGONS

Every now and then, on railway platforms in the southern half of England, I have encountered what seems like an apparition from another age, passing by before the bleared eyes have had a chance to focus on it. Somehow, it always chooses the moment when the traveller's spirit has sunk to its lowest in the personal thermometer – such as when you are waiting to come home, after an aborted breakfast, from somewhere you wish you'd never been, or when you are waiting between connections, at a junction you have never heard of, while proceeding to somewhere you wonder whether anybody ever really needs to go.

No matter what is registered on the station clock (and last week at Victoria, three of them were giving different times, carefully arranged to be just far enough apart to cause the maximum panic for the minimum error) this ghost train manages to give the impression of gliding out of dawn or into dusk, that magic hour of change when all souls long to be on the move, preferably being served with food and drink by somebody else.

Like a Japanese scroll, it unrolls, this opulent, cream-and-brown, Art Deco strip, flashing a glimpse of wood panelling as polished as wax fruit; gilded fittings out of a Mayfair Arab's bathroom; tented lamps, miniature cities of bottles; silver trays floating, with only a severed hand to support them, in mid-air; and the passengers, wispy cut-outs slightly blurred, background revellers in a glossy ad.

It could be a flashback, an unironed-out wrinkle in the time-warp, a *déjà-vu* recall of a classic travel poster. Why – it might even be the Orient Express! Now, having just been wandering around Kent aboard it, I realise that is what it is. Well, almost.

'Orient Express' is one of those names which can make even those totally immune to the Romance of Steam go a little soft in the head, 'loco-loco' as it is known among American railway buffs. I usually lodge it in my own informal hierarchy just after the front-runner, the Trans-Siberian, and noticeably ahead of those schoolboy swing-time favourites, the Chattanooga Choochoo, and the Atchison, Topeka and the Sante Fe. I used to imagine it as a single unique conveyance, coupled up around a hundred years ago for the first time, and running on and off, with gaps for wars and depressions, until recently. Now I have learned that the title covered various other regular services, criss-crossing Europe, which possessed names almost as evocative – Rome Express, Train Bleu, Nord Express, Flèche d'Or, Sud Express, Oiseau Bleu, Edelweiss Express. I could swear I had read the book and seen the film of all of them.

The daddy of them all, the first Orient Express, steamed out of the Gare de l'Est in Paris on the 4th of October, 1883, carrying passengers for Constantinople. The de luxe new Wagon-Lit coaches, mounted on special patent bogies guaranteed to permit a gentleman to shave even at speeds of 80 kilometres an hour, went only as far as Giurgi, on the Romanian bank of the Danube. From then on, you reverted to antiquated Austrian rolling stock, later transferring to a ferry for a usually unsettling 18-hour sea trip. It was not until 1889 that the '*Compagnie Internationale des Wagon-Lits et des Grands Express Européens*' was able to take you all the way on a journey that lasted 67 hours and 35 minutes.

Even then, you might hit an occasional bout of turbulence when King Boris III of Bulgaria exercised the ancient, traditional prerogative he had just invented by climbing into the cab and personally driving the locomotive across his territory.

But what the world thinks of as the Orient Express, with its swanky derivatives, was invented, designed and constructed in the Twenties and Thirties. Those cars which still remain are listed and catalogued like Old Masters. What happened to them during the last war could in itself make a curious memoir. 3309 carried on running inside Germany, while 3425 operated out of Istanbul into the Balkans. 3539 was stored in Paris while 3482 and 3552 were used as hotels in Lyons. 4110 was stored in Bucharest while 3674 ran around German-occupied France.

Several were kept at sidings in Lourdes while 3544 was turned into a brothel in Limoges. The most historic of them all was 2419, in which Marshal Foch insisted the Germans signed the Armistice at Compiègne in 1918 – a compliment reciprocated by Hitler when he forced the French to surrender on the same spot, on board train, in 1940.

After the last war, attempts were made to revive *les Grands Express*, and versions of them lingered on as late as 1977 (Costa Brava Express). I wish I could say I had caught a recognisable one. The nearest I came was in the early Seventies when I joined what the Orient Express had then become, a single car, to cross Northern Italy. It happened to be the week of a general strike, and despite having paid first-class, with special surcharge, and booked a seat, I had to stand all the way in the corridor on one leg (the other was folded back on my suitcase) glowering vainly at two fat peasant women who occupied my place, impregnable behind the baskets of heat-exhausted chickens.

What had marked the Orient was the elegant, high-camp style in which its cars were decorated, the first time that public transport had set out, sparing no expense, to provide what had previously been available only in the private quarters of millionaires and monarchs. James Sherwood, President of Sea Containers, acquired some of the last remaining cars at a sale in Monte Carlo in 1977. Now, buffed up and restored, they are in their third year as the Venice Simplon Orient-Express, running from London down to Florence.

There is something slightly sickening, to my mind, about the publicity materials (I haven't tried the reality) of this enterprise. In a period of depression and unemployment on a massive scale, it seems rather crass, not to say somehow mentally-backward, to place such an emphasis on the superiority of a great number of products simply because they are the most expensive.

In the brochure given to all Europe-bound passengers, there is a series of pictures showing the progress of a traveller from platform to sitting-room to desk to bar to table to wash-basin to bed. You might imagine this was, as often in hotels, to show you the facilities available, with perhaps a touch of managerial self-satisfaction. Not so.

Turn on and you will see the same photographs, now reduced to numbered outlines, like group portraits in the old *Tatler*, demonstrating that you can buy every single item you have seen or touched. Ashtray, brass, 6" × 6" – £29.50. Tea-cup and saucer, in blue or brown – £13.50. Ice bucket, Art Nouveau design, silver-plated – £120. Passport/Jotter – £47.50.

The V.S.O-E version of the Orient Express which wanders round southern Britain is not quite so stunningly identified with a *hig-lef*, *de luxe*, E Phillips Oppenheim/Joseph Sternberg existence most of us thought the rich had been forbidden by their doctors to follow any more.

This was nearer the old, familiar, admirable Pullman that I do remember using as the Brighton Belle or the Queen of Scots, in itself exuding a degree of solid, pleasant comfort that nobody who became used to it is likely to underrate. Though I must say I was surprised to find I had forgotten some of the nicer touches – did they always have a stained-glass window, a marble sink and a mosaic floor, in the lavatory? There is something reassuring about solid brass luggage racks, and coat-hangers, over-head, though they are clearly built for the minimum impedimenta carried by the really important. (The Orient Express attracted its distinctive customers not only by announcing that it was the first trans-European service where Customs and Immigration formalities were performed on board, but by offering to carry for each traveller, in the guard's van of course, up to 23 stones of baggage free.) But my own favourite advantage which this possesses over the best of British Rail is that you have the individual, movable, wing arm-chair of your own, an assertion of separate identity worth a sizeable extra fee.

Given back their old shine and sheen, these rail-cars are hired out by Sherwood's V.S.O-E organisation to run up-market excursions around the bottom half of these islands. Mostly they occur in Southern Region of BR, between 8 am and 6 pm, since it is not easy to insert this strange outsider at short notice into the immensely complex, computerised network. Longer expeditions do occur – not long since I saw one, blazing through the darkness, near Liverpool – stop-ping overnight, but only midweek and in certain months.

I suppose the usual hirers are really fat-cat companies or posh quangos – though the information booklets suggest that a fee varying between £8,000 and £16,000 is not exorbitant for what they describe as 'an original and unique way of entertaining *friends*, business colleagues and clients.' My italics. Whose friends?

My first experience of this facility was on a day's outing organised by the Apple and Pear Development Council, and thoroughly enjoyable it all was, in the baking heat under the scented boughs, where the fruit rested, cosy yet supported, in your hands like – I have to say it because it's true – like a woman's breasts. What it might have felt like to the women journalists present, it is up to them to say.

On board the jolly train, champagne and apple juice was the alternative to champagne, as an early-morn aperitif (most of the food correspondents, no doubt on health grounds, refused the apple juice), I overheard some discussion by expert, veteran publicists as to whether this kind of operation was really worth the time and expense involved. Then they fell to measuring other possible means

'*Aye, but this is the Cairngorms, laddie . . . that'll be one pound and fifteen pence!*'

of interesting the British public in home-grown produce.

'Kenneth Williams wanted twenty thou ...' said one.

'What!' sputtered another.

'Spike wanted thirty ...'

'I'm so glad I signed up Daley before he won his gold,' breathed another.

As for me, I must admit I might not have joined the outing, except for two names, and they weren't 'apples' and 'pears'. They were Venice Simplon Orient-Express, and champagne. And I was glad I went.

As a British apple-lover, I needed little convincing. But I was glad to be told that the foreign competition, Golden Delicious, is dumped here before it is ripe, when it would be sweeter and yellower as befits its name. I was interested to learn that the main opposition to our apples is from the young who have developed an appetite for conformity and regularity that encourages them to reject any fruit with odd bumps or variable complexions. And I sensed that with Discovery, a red and conventional-looking variety, British growers were trying to provide the equivalent of Golden Delicious in another shade.

Nothing will shake me from Cox's Orange but I was impressed by my orchard tour, especially since the farmer was determined not to seem to be ingratiating himself with the well-irrigated hacks. He took us round with the air of Field-Marshal Montgomery shepherding a herd of pacifists about El Alamein.

'Keep up at the back there ... If you want to speak perhaps you'd like to tell us all about it ... I wish I had more time to explain, but we're working here.' And he also deployed a good propaganda line – conscious that some of us, including my good-self, had been helping the enemy by spreading alarm and despondency about chemical residues in food, he showed us the one apple-tree in the acres of orchard that looked grey and withered, as if stricken by the Messiah. When we had finished commiserating, he said, 'That was the only one that was *not* sprayed.'

On the way back, lobster salad, champagne, claret, I remembered I had snitched a Discovery. I bit into it; though not golden, it was delicious. I'm sold. But then so I would have been if I had never moved further than the Oxford Road fruit stall in Kentish Town. Wouldn't I?

29.8.1984

'I could only afford the one week!'

LARRY'S PISTE

Hunter Davies

SKI'S THE LIMIT

Well here we are, Mum, back from our ski holiday, all limbs intact, numbered and correct, glowing with pride and perhaps the slightest hint of a tan, or maybe too much *glühwein*. We did it. We survived. Only my wallet took a battering.

How does the rest of the world manage it? The money, I mean. Munich Airport yesterday was like the Kop end. I can understand all those middle-thirties school teachers and secretaries of indeterminate sex, saving up all year for their annual blow-out, but where do the yobboes get the dosh from? I asked a hooligan as we queued for the duty free which for once, you won't believe this, included something which was free. They were giving away sample glasses of Dewar's. Really. Munich Airport. That dump.

Anyway, I got talking to this lad in jeans and T-shirt, which looked as if he'd slept in them all week, together with two black eyes, and he said he went skiing every January, plus Majorca in the summer. 'I'm in the SAS,' he said. 'But don't tell anyone.'

Oh, you get some jokers on the slopes, though all week we only came across the more refined version. We were staying at Alpbach, a terribly genteel place in the Tyrol, very popular with middle-class families. Naturally, we were in the best and nicest hotel, the Böglerhof. We don't mess about. My MI5 salary is quite good these days.

As usual, the hardest thing to survive on any ski holiday was the first day. Make a mess of that and you might as well go straight home. We all had to assemble at a certain point first thing on Monday morning to get ourselves graded like Sainsbury's eggs. It was chaos. One thousand lame ducks were milling around, convinced their boots didn't fit and that they'd been given the wrong skis, feeling stupid in their new clothes and wondering if it would have been safer to have gone sky-diving. It reminded me of the first day in the Army.

OK, Mum, so I haven't been in the Army. The first day at a new school. I went to lots of those. Who will be my new friend? Will we get that strict teacher? Will I ever know my way around this strange place? What if I don't understand *anything*? And yes, these boots are definitely killing me. I'll have to take them back to the museum at lunchtime. John Glenn will be needing them.

It was easy for Flora, never having skied before. She stood at the post marked 'five', for beginner children, while all around the fantasists slithered on the snow in their C & A salopettes. I had gone skiing once before, though it was six years ago. Surely I can't have forgotten anything. I'm so much older and wiser these days. Jake had also skied once before, last year with the school. He was convinced he was the new Franz Klammer, but I persuaded him that we should both try for group four, adults, the second stage up in the hierarchy. Top people, those legendary sixth-form skiers, the Flash Harry Evanses, are in group one.

We had to ski down this slope, all we presumptive group four types, in full view of the whole world, while this very bossy garden gnome in red, one of the chief instructors, told us where to go. If he's an expert, so I thought, with that belly, there's a chance for me yet, but of course the thing about skiing is that you can't tell by physique who's got the knack. No wonder all those school-teachers love it. They wouldn't dare strip off in Benidorm but with their goggles on they could be Brigitte Bardot.

Now, this is the bit which led to some heated argument. Jake and I were put in different classes, both grade four classes, but I maintain mine was the *better* class. Stands to reason. Did I fall over? Did I heckers. OK then, Jake, neither did you, but I could tell by the Gnome's voice that he thought my class was higher. S'obvious.

In the end, though, Jake was the clear winner. I never felt I progressed during the whole week. Naturally, I'm blaming our Instructor. That's what Instructors are for. Get an Open Scholarship to Balliol and of course it was your own innate cleverness. Fail all your O-levels and certainly it was the fault of that stupid school. Those rotten teachers. They never did any stretching.

We were fourteen in our class for a start, which was far too many. Ten of them were German, so the Instructor spoke their language most of the time. I learned a lot of German but never managed a parallel turn. He wouldn't stay on the baby drag lifts, which me and the three other yellow-bellied Brits wanted, but insisted on taking us down ice-bound mountain slopes. Each day was a survival test. Follow me, he said, and disappeared off the edge of the world.

Two days before the end of the week we played truant and left him. We then did a lot of sun-bathing and had some long lunches and pretended we were on holiday at last, not at an Outward Bound penitentiary.

Jake and Flora both had excellent teachers and progressed very well and I often saw them, whizzing down the hard stuff while I was snow ploughing through my second apple strudel. I made friends with this bloke called John from Kent who is in the *Guinness Book of Records* as his family building firm dates back to 1591, making it the oldest private company in the country. So he said. I must check this, next time I'm in the library. Perhaps *he* was really in the SAS.

They didn't, of course, speak to me, did Jake and Flora, though I shouted after them in my best German. Benzeeneezanzeeankels. It was my clothes, you see. I stuck to my vow not to buy any ski clothes whatsoever, determined to stamp out all ski suit manufacturers. I later learned from one of the Germans in our class that they always

referred to me as the Poor Engländer, the One Who Can't Afford Any Clothes. Cheeky sods.

Most days I wore my old track suit and football socks, plus several layers underneath, and was never wet and never cold, even going up on the chair lift to the top of the Sillyburgerhof mountain, though the tips of my fingers, inside my Marks and Spencer gloves, once did get a bit chilly. When I fell, which I did regularly, then of course I had to brush off the snow very quickly. One day it snowed, so I got out my waterproof leggings, the baggy dark green ones I wear in the Lake District for walking, and my 1960s blue plastic top. That was when the rest of the family refused to acknowledge me. What a jerk, they all said. Glad he's not with us.

I just smiled, in my superior way, at those one thousand brain-washed, image obsessed suckers who had lashed out a fortune on unnecessary ski clothes. One day in the restaurant I picked up a *Daily Mail*, after all the Germans had gone to queue jump, and saw that Koo Stark had paid £170 to get fitted up for a ski hol. Well, she would, wouldn't she.

The Après Ski was rather jolly, well organised by Global, the firm we went with. The best thing was probably the Tyrolean evening which Flora maintained was called the Terylene evening. There should be a Nylon Night or a Polythene Party.

Everyone always has to go to one of these folksy evenings, otherwise you haven't been skiing. That's when the locals slap each other's bare thighs in their short leather trousers and pretend to chop wood or yodel and generally jump around looking stupid. Jake was convinced it was Monty Python. Every dance seemed the same to me, though each time it was preceded by a different but very lengthy introduction. One dance was supposed to be about love-sick mountain maids having love-sick mountain lads tapping at their windows, then they all came on and went through the same thigh-slapping routine. Flora loved it.

Then there was a sleigh ride and a fondue party, though my wife refused to go to this. She maintains that fondues are for people who don't like food. Quite right. It's as pointless as dressing up for skiing, all image making and equipment using, except in this case you end up smelling like a chip shop. I loved it. We don't get chips at home.

So, Mum, we've all come back with fondue memories and the whole family wants to go again next year, even Jake. He was only slightly put out when an English girl in his group, whose Christian name was China, asked him if he was embarrassed being called Jake. Flora maintains that her class was upgraded during the week from a Five to a Four. Show-off. As for me, I think I might invest in some ski mittens next time. Not for the slopes, as I might just stick to walking, which was what my lady wife did, but for the fondue. Bloody hot, those fondue sticks.

19.1.1983

Laurie Taylor

WHAT'S YOUR INSIDE LEG?

I'm having some slight trouble with my Inner Voice – you know, that critical little ego which creeps up on you when you're setting out for a quick game of doubles in Battersea Park and whispers such things as, 'Well, who do we think we are, then? All dressed up in our Adidas finery and multi-coloured sweat-bands. Pity, though, about the bandy legs.'

I'd always rather assumed that others around me were similarly plagued: that the Inner Voice was one of those features of life, much like my wife's predilection for saying 'sort of', which had to be borne with good grace. That is, until last month when I stumbled across the manuscript, to be published by Fernhurst Books, of an absolutely splendid work on skiing by a Mr Peter Lightfoot.

Mr Lightfoot (who runs courses at Ski Skills, 12 Ranelagh Road, Redhill, Surrey) is one of those advocates of a completely new approach to games and sports in which you keep well away from the sport itself until you're certain that your mental attitude is perfectly right. Instead of clipping on your skis and setting off down the sides of mountains desperately trying to remember the instructions, you first of all sit at home, or in some cases stand on one leg (but I'll be coming to that in a moment) and develop the appropriate frame of mind. Or as my wife put it succinctly this morning, 'the appropriate sort of frame of mind'.

Now Mr Lightfoot is a modest man, but he obviously believes, with something approaching a religious fervour, that most people's attitude to skiing, whether they be experts or beginners, is quite wrong. Neither will he have it that some of us are natural skiers and others genetic stumblebums. Right from the outset, he insists that we're all born to ski. It is only a question of bringing out our hidden talent. As he nicely puts it: 'We arrive on this planet with as much potential within us to be a skier as does the acorn have the potential within itself to become an imposing oak tree.'

And this is where the Inner Voice comes in. Or rather goes out. For Mr Lightfoot strongly believes that you will never learn to ski successfully, or improve on your present modest performance, if every time you slip on your reflective glasses, that Inner Voice starts asking what you look like, or deciding if you're doing well, or – and in this, I must admit, I'm going slightly beyond Mr Lightfoot's examples – wondering what on earth could possibly be the point of spending hours of one's finite existence sliding down the side of a mountain and then promptly returning to the top to repeat the exercise.

So what is to be done? Well, argues Mr Lightfoot in his thoroughly readable prose – nothing heavy-handed, or heavy-footed, about Mr Lightfoot – the only way to silence that terrible ego is to let your body assert itself. Trust your body. And in truth, even those like myself, who trust only parts of their bodies (I have always entertained deep suspicions about the general commitment of my legs), will find encouragement from sections whose titles intriguingly combine the anatomy lesson and the encounter group: 'Undo those boots,' 'Looking at our hands,' 'The laser beam in your fingertips,' 'Focusing in on the hips,' 'Take a look at our pelvis.'

And to assist such self-examination there are dozens of practical little experiments. If we try one together it will help to make the general point. Ready? 'Stand up, close your eyes, and lift one foot six inches off the floor.' It's all a bit wobbly, isn't it? I'll pop into capitals for a second to make it easier for you to follow the next bit. 'START TO BE AWARE OF THE MANY MUSCLE MOVEMENTS IN THE FOOT SUPPORTING YOUR WEIGHT.' Getting steadier now? Right. 'Then transfer your attention to the foot in the air and notice the way it is moving slightly, acting as a balancing weight.'

You see what happened, don't you? (YES, DO PUT YOUR FOOT DOWN.) You were so involved in simply standing on one leg that the nasty Inner Voice retreated. 'Our little voices were not evident at all, not advising, not criticising, not judging, not teaching. Where were they? They had the responsibility of being totally aware of the forces acting on the body – there was no desire to interfere.'

I'm only too pleased if that's the way it worked for you. You're obviously ready for the next exercises which appear to take place on Tube trains and park roundabouts. But,

speaking personally, I have to admit to a slight problem with this technique. Although I've spent several weeks now on this preliminary experiment, albeit moving round the house to add a little interest and occasionally changing legs, I still seem to find it quite unreasonably difficult to stand in the middle of a room on one foot without hearing my Inner Voice asking – quite forcefully, really – 'What on earth do you think you're doing standing in the middle of a room on one foot?'

None of this reflects on the excellent Mr Lightfoot. Call it Sartrean if you will, but there is something about the mundane which has always brought out the philosopher in me. Other people have to climb mountains with lovers and stare hard into the setting sun before getting at all bothered about the insignificance of their own being, but I can get utterly overtaken by the profoundest ontological doubts when pulling dental floss between my molars.

It might be, of course, that anxieties are getting in the way of my body's natural expression. Mr Lightfoot is as always ready to step in and do something about this sort of problem before he allows his pupils out on their own. 'I draw a circle in the snow with my stick,' he tells us, 'I then invite anyone who is anxious, concerned, worried, distracted or disappointed by ANYTHING to step forward and state the distraction, and by stabbing at the circle with their ski-sticks leave it behind.'

Excellent. That's obviously the way to do it. I'd certainly welcome a chance to get my orthodontal anxieties out there in the snow with a ski-stick through them. Then, after a couple of healthy stabs at the imminence of the thermonuclear holocaust, and perhaps a final lunge at my wife's 'sort of's', I'd be as ready as anyone for the off-piste.

Once I do get on those actual slopes I know that I will also be helped along greatly by Mr Lightfoot's advanced body games: there is, for example, exhaling while making noises like waves crashing against the rocks, pretending to be a cat, imagining that I'm in the middle of a hula-hoop, and making absolutely certain that I'm 'in' my boots rather than merely 'on' them. (A common failing, apparently.) And what's more, all these little games will prevent us getting bored with our skiing. In the words of a mature student: 'Sipping a last *Glühwein* before skiing the final section of the run to Zermatt, I felt I had recaptured the excitement and enjoyment of my first week as a beginner.'

In fact it's all so refreshingly inspirational, so far away from all those tedious books of rote instructions, that I know that once I can crack this problem of the Inner Voice I'll be championship material. I've worked out my programme of personal development with great care. Stage by stage. In fact, in precisely that rational form you'd expect from someone who, whatever the height of his ultimate skiing ambition, still has one foot planted firmly on the ground.

16.1.1985

Dorothy Stannard

EAU DE NILE

According to the languid bidding of a man reclining on a carpet in the Luxor bazaar, I am worth 3 million camels. Not an inconsiderable number, you must agree. But then the boys here will tell you anything, especially if they're trying to sell you a chipped head of Nefertiti wrapped in newspaper or a factory-made scarab 'from the tomb of Tutankhamen'.

'Queen Hatshepsut (*Pharaoh, tyrant and temple builder: a compliment any feminist would be proud of*), your skin is like the moon, your eyes they are stars, ten postcards for a pound.'

'Picture with Michael, signora?' Michael is a camel named after Michael Jackson. Great sense of humour, the Egyptians. Even in high summer on the Nile.

But nobody goes in summer, darling, it's far too hot, they tell you back home. In fact, summer is an excellent time to go, precisely because no one else is there. Only the very best sort of traveller braves temperatures of 120° in Upper Egypt: 'Goddess Hathor' from Australia, named after the cow-faced goddess of Dendera and proud of it; 'Beau Geste' of South London; and Sue from Sheffield, mistress of the petal-edged doily, to name but a few of our party. Between us we are equipped with an artificial leg, a glass eye, three inhalers and four telescopic umbrellas: the kind of kit that comes in handy 600 miles up the Nile.

A 17-day cruise down the Nile with Swan Hellenic, a division of that British institution, the P and O, has elements of the Grand Tour still. Enough indeed to send alarm bells ringing through a democratic breast: but there is no vulgar swimming-pool or disco, and there is an Egyptology and ornithology library and a same-day laundry service. While you always find one or two people who seem surgically strapped to double gins and Jeffrey Archer novels, the general spirit aboard the *Nile Star* is wholesome – a little unadventurous and worried about lurking dysentery and malaria, but good-natured and well-behaved.

Since this is a cultural tour, at 6.30 each evening we troop into the lounge for a lecture and slide show from our resident Egyptologist; 'This evening's lecture on the development of the step pyramid in Sakkara begins with the primordial mound ...' Zzzzz. Make a note never to sit next to Bill again. Bill's chin sinks on to his chest and his mouth drops ajar to emit a soft snoring sound. He is on his thirtieth cruise and has been there and done it all already.

Others doze more politely, their eyes closing behind dark glasses in that delicious half-sleep that follows a full day and cocktails on deck; the mysteries of the step pyramid mix with memories of loofah stalls and date palms or the image of Goddess Nut spanning the starry roof of a tomb. Sue usually crotchets, while anyone actually alert scribbles notes with blunted pencils, ballpoints having been thrown to children on the quayside and then thrust deep into *gallabayas* along with boiled sweets and Polo mints.

'*Stylo, stylo,*' the children shout. Our passengers' grasp of French is not great and though the children mime their demands with Marcel Marceau-type scribbling movements, they are thrown all manner of unsatisfactory items – freshen-up, cologne-impregnated tissues and sachets of shampoo from the Rameses Hilton, Cairo – before someone remembers the English translation.

These exchanges at the barrages and bridges prompt discussion about begging, the consensus seeming to be that doling out sweets and baubles, darling (for the women are most guilty), only encourages it. Actually, there seems to be little begging in Egypt these days. No doubt in the stews of Cairo and Alexandria, where Swan Hellenic angels fear to tread, proper beggars exist, and in parts of the country, particularly in the much tramped-over Valleys of the Kings, Queens and Nobles, an infant's first words may be English: 'very cheap', accompanied by one raised finger. But in my whole trip I see just a single beggar.

What really gets everyone going, though, even more than the pros and cons of the Aswan Dam, is the fellahs' use of animals. A donkey may be so overburdened by sugarcane that it totters more precariously than an adolescent in stilettos. On the other hand out in the fields it grazes freely while its poor owner stoops and struggles: and if we didn't choose the horse with the toast-rack ribs to pull our carriage into town, well, then it would never get fed, would it? This is the Third World for gawd's sake.

The real question to me was: how much we would see of Egypt from a flat-out position between the irrigated flower-tubs on deck and our air-conditioned cabins below? Did the youthful blond-haired crowd alighting from the felucca at Luxor, who paid eight pounds each to travel from Aswan, and ate, slept and sunbathed as they sailed, penetrate Egypt more deeply? I doubt it – not dressed like that.

The rest of us don't do too badly. When it comes to the ancient archaeological sites – Abu Simbel, Philae, Kom-Ombo, Karnak, Thebes, Dendera, Sakkara, Memphis, Gizeh – we are experts compared with the average Egyptian. By the end of our trip even our Americans are hacking across a Coptic rubbish dump, circa A.D. 400, with nonchalance, considering it all rather recent. Most of populated Egypt can be seen very easily from a boat, since the strips of fertile land, where most of the 47 million live, are confined to a few miles either side of the Nile.

There are loads of opportunities to absorb Egypt and you start to feel you have sorted out your preconceptions from your flashes of great insight. Until, that is, an Egyptian companion, a man who is an opera lover and Rembrandt admirer and who has the faultless taste to choose for swimming Luxor's nineteenth-century Winter Palace, one of Egypt's few surviving grand hotels, rather than the popular modern Etap, suddenly suspends conversation and swivels 180° at the stir of a blonde in a bikini. Typical Mediterranean machismo or another instance of that faultless taste?

And was that really a Saudi prince in the Marriott Hotel, Cairo? Diamond or rhinestone on the middle finger of his right hand? 'Two-a-penny, Saudi princes, darling, not the same thing at all as a Royal,' I am told. Even so, a prince! Can you imagine Charles inviting a couple of strangers up for a Coca-Cola in his suite?

Day 15: we wind up back at Cairo. A canapé-throw away from the *Nile Star*, the rest of Cairo is pure madness – a huge building site loud with the 24-hour cacophony of car horns. To a population still newly used to the motorcar, peeping the horn is considered an entertainment. But it is way back in Islington two days later that I am stopped three times for baksheesh on a one-way stroll down Upper Street.

21.1.1987

Robert Morley

SETTLING THE ELEPHANT BILL

'I am a little closer to the herd than I would have wished,' Mr Sutchbury, the white tracker in chief at The Bumi Hills Safari Lodge, informed me, 'so it would help me if you were to ignore them.' I gave my celebrated impersonation of a waiter in Leningrad confronted by a customer.

'How did I do,' I asked a few breathless moments later.

'Very well indeed,' Mr Sutchbury – perhaps we should call him Jeff like everyone else – told me.

'You noticed perhaps,' I went on, considerably encouraged, 'that I looked through and not at them. It is no good simply averting one's gaze.'

But I no longer had Jeff's attention. He had climbed from the Jeep and was enthusiastically examining the spoor of a water buffalo. How my mother would have hated this preoccupation with game droppings. A careless walker in my youth, I was so often chided for stepping in something nasty. In point of fact, that morning we never did find the buffalo but later Jeff, temporarily at a loss to point out an impala leaping ahead or a crocodile lagging behind, presented me with a sample of dried elephant dung and, extracting a hard stone from the centre, invited my diagnosis. A small elephant gallstone, I hazarded.

'Think,' admonished my teacher. 'That is not the way one passes a gallstone. No, this is the kernel of a local plum and if you care to retain and polish it and hang it round your neck it makes a powerful talisman.'

'We're doing all right at the moment,' I reassured, 'no need for ju-ju. How about luncheon then?'

Later that evening I rather wished I'd taken his advice. We were finishing an elaborate meal in the dining-room when a Japanese guest approached Jeff and with some hesitation opined there was an elephant on the rampage. White hunters have considerable charisma; they are indeed closely akin to ski instructors in the idolatry they inspire in their clients. The Japanese lady was clearly apprehensive at disturbing his meal.

'Will be with you in a moment,' Jeff told her, 'don't go too near.' However, the sherry trifle had to be abandoned as the elephant started to test the chlorine content of the pool. Game reserve denizens are as anxious as anyone to see the guests are comfortable and up to strength, otherwise they might once again be at the mercy of the poaching community.

Jeff spoke sharply to the enormous pachyderm and he gracefully retreated through the garden and stepped daintily over walls constructed with the sole purpose of excluding him. Later, however, he reappeared and stood blocking the path to my individual chalet-style bedroom. We had already had several nightcaps but Jeff advised we should return to the bar and wait till the beast had finished demolishing the bougainvillaea, a great delicacy to elephants, apparently.

'I think,' I told Jeff, 'there might be just room to sidle past,' while of course taking his advice to ignore him.

'He'd kill you,' he told me.

'In that case I might squeeze past and give him a friendly pat on the rump wishing him a peaceful night.' It was not, of course, a serious suggestion and a few minutes later Charles, such was his name, had wandered back to his club or wherever elephants spend the evening.

I was awake at dawn; if I have one complaint about hotels in Zimbabwe, it is the curtains are seldom thick enough, otherwise everything is *Haut Luxe*, to use one of the two phrases my father ever uttered in the French tongue, the other being *Le Bon Dieu*. 'I believe', he frequently affirmed, 'in Le Bon Dieu and feel no need to go to church, at least on this side of the Channel.'

Leaving my father aside for the moment and returning to Bumi, pronounced as if spelt with a double 'O', we took several trips by boat and Jeep along the shore of Lake Kariba, the enormous artificial lake caused by the damming of the Zambezi, on the trail of lion, zebra, leopard, hyena, honey badger or banded mongoose. You can't, of course, win them all and when I came to my score card, thoughtfully provided in my room along with the laundry list, I was rather discouraged to note how few of the odd two hundred animals listed I could truthfully claim. About a dozen if I was honest, which I wasn't. It's always better not to hang about in the sun too long. If Jeff spotted a grysbok, that counted in my book too.

'Marvellous,' I would observe and secretly wonder what the creature might have looked like if I too had managed to spot it browsing on a thorn bush. I am not a glutton for game, except for the occasional grouse or partridge, and although I was invited to taste crocodile, apparently always in season in Zimbabwe, I resisted the offer. Tough as old boots, I imagine, which they often indeed are made into.

The building of the dam and the consequent flooding of the valley in which at one time 57,000 Tonga tribesmen fished and farmed and had to be rescued along with hundreds of species of snakes, birds, beasts and butterflies, delayed for some time the inauguration of the Kariba Prawn Farm, which now fortunately is in full production but such is the demand at home as well as abroad for these superlative crustaceans that they are not always easy to come by.

Having apparently exhausted the local supply, we moved on to glimpse the Victoria Falls, 'the smoke that thunders' as it was called before Livingstone canoed cautiously downstream and wisely disembarked in time.

They stretch for nearly a mile and are nowadays reached by a footpath from the Victoria Falls Hotel, another splendid establishment operated currently by the Zimbabwe Sun Hotels but with a history going back for nearly 100 years when the Falls first became a tourist attraction and luxury trains were operated four times a year from Cape Town for the pleasure of our ancestors and the enrichment of the local citizens who originally founded a settlement, which soon had to be abandoned, on the opposite bank of the great river. The Old Drift, as it was called, boasted an all-night bar complete with roulette wheel and full-time croupier, but so large a proportion of the players succumbed to Black Water Fever that the traders, trappers and gamblers eventually moved off to higher ground.

The guidebook is at pains to reassure that this and other diseases prevalent in Livingstone Days have been either wiped out completely or kept under control. Visitors are, however, advised to take an anti-malarial

'I felt a bit sorry for him after I shot his elephant.'

tablet once a week and because the hippos and crocodiles are still around, completely desist from bathing or paddling except in the swimming pools. It adds that bites from insects are so rare as to be hardly worth mentioning but in cases of doubt the local pharmacist will be pleased to help. Luckily the casinos have survived, although the most elegant was unfortunately burnt to the ground in the recent conflict. A ground-to-air missile, launched from the Zambian side of the river, mistook it, on account of the heat engendered by its air-conditioning plant, for the aeroplane at which it was launched.

In Harare, which was until recently called Salisbury, there is, since the Government raised basic wages all along the line, a temporary shortage of dairy products – not, of course, experienced by the tourist hotels. There is considerable theatrical activity and I was able to attend a school performance of *A Ghost on Tiptoe*. I have always thought this was the worst play I ever wrote but thanks to the brilliance of the cast have now decided it was my masterpiece. If it is not to be revived in the West End, I live in hopes that Kariba Prawns at least will soon make their appearance on the shelves of my local supermarket.

29.9.1982

'Who is it to-day – ITV or BBC?'

Ronald Searle

Alex Atkinson

ESCAPE WITH MRS DYSON

At Home with Aborigines

When it comes to a question of really intensive fieldwork, carried out on the spot over a period of months or even years, one of the bitterest sources of disappointment for anthropologists to-day – apart from their steadily growing conviction that people all over the world are becoming more numerous, less different, and far dirtier – is the fact that there are hardly any quaint tribes left now who are prepared to extend hospitality indefinitely to a lot of subsidised professors with jeeps and notebooks.

'I might fit a party of three in for a week or so next February,' wrote the Chief of a tribe of unusual giants in Borneo,* to whom Mrs Dyson had applied for digs, 'but more than that I cannot promise. This place has been overrun with anthropologists during the last few years. They come here, insist on living as we do, eat us out of house and home, put ideas into our heads, take no active part in hunting or tree-felling, throw doubts on the validity and even the originality of our religion, complain about the sanitation, accuse us of having rickets, take flash-light photos during our Saturday night fertility rites, and generally disturb the even tenor of existence. Then they go home and put us into encyclopædias, and we don't make a brass farthing out of it. I remain yours etc.'

You will therefore readily understand Mrs Dyson's delight when we found the astonishing Mugus† in their mountain fastness deep in the interior of the largest of the three islands that form the Cocoranga Group, not very far from New Zealand, and were told, after a surprisingly brief parley, that we could stay as long as we liked provided that we promise never to divulge the secret password ('*Um t'ala groh*,' which means 'Long is the claw of the land crab').

Mrs Dyson had always felt confident that there were Mugus to be found on this particular island, chiefly on account of those intriguing references in Farringdon's *Chronicle of My Journeying In the Southern Oceans, With Some Accompt of Witches* to 'men of but little tallnesse who, hauing no tools saue only mallets of stone and a kinde of wheel Barrow, yet raise up great Dwellings in the forest of this isle, where they do liue and thriue mightily.' Farringdon's grasp of geography understandably left much to be desired, and for years controversy has raged about the exact location of his isle; but Mrs Dyson never wavered in her belief that the Cocoranga Group was the place, quoting as her proof the following passage in the *Chronicle:*—

Whereupon we did mooue forward in such small winde as did preuail from the Eastwards; altho we greatly doubted that our Mastes would long remain upright,

---

* For the English translation of this letter I am indebted to Llewellyn Carfax of Hunstanton.

† Pronounced to rhyme with 'fingers.'

being made fraile by the Storm; and in this sort we went onward. Now when we had trauelled three leags vpon our course, we did espy the greatest of the three Isles, being in the Middle, and in Shape like a Pidgeon, the head and Beake lying to the North, the rump and Taile at the South. Drawing neare, and hauing no longer any terrour that Worse might befall us, we did ground the Galley on the shore, and marching boldly forward, did meet at once a Company of strange Human creatures; who did fall vpon and eat Two of our number before we had made ready our Fowling pieces. In this and in diuers other matters they did shew such inciuility that we were presently resolued not to remain long in their midst, but to spy out whether there might be space here for a new Colony, and then depart.

'This is the place all right,' said Mrs Dyson, as we lurched up on to the beach in the surplus assault landing craft she had wheedled out of some anthropology-lover on the mainland. 'You couldn't hope for a more pigeon-shaped isle. Now all we have to do is to poke about until we find the most inaccessible district there is. That's where the Mugus will be, you take my tip – otherwise some fool would have stumbled across them long before this. Well now, first of all we'd better have a roll-call and a brew-up.'

There were five of us in the party. Mrs Dyson's own main functions were to form irrevocable conclusions from the tentative findings of her experts, and to take the credit for whatever astounding scientific discoveries we were able to foist on to the public when we got back home. ('I may not be any great shakes as an anthropologist myself,' she had said, 'but *I* found the backers for this trip, and if anybody gets anything out of the Nuffield Trust or the *Reader's Digest* on the strength of it, it's going to be me.' One of the backers, by the way, was a man named Harper who wanted us to try out a foolproof apparatus he had invented for snaring rhino,

and when I pointed out to Mrs Dyson that as we weren't likely to come within a thousand miles of any rhino it smacked a little of sharp practice to take the fellow's money, she said 'Not at all. As a matter of fact it makes a very good hammock, and he'll probably become a millionaire as a result of my recommendation. Think of it – *Mrs Dyson Sleeps On This Harper Hammock – Why Don't You?* After all, more people sleep on hammocks than snare rhino.' – 'Yes,' I said, 'but not *many* more'.) Then there was a very old man by the name of Rossiter, whose special subject was somatology and who had to be helped up hills on account of his bones. He said they were brittle. Edwin Bothe was described on his passport as an ethnologist and once, in the course of his investigations, he had unfortunately been converted to animism by some people in Central Africa, which made him rather jumpy. On the other hand, as Mrs Dyson was always quick to point out in his defence, he was a good plain cook and never threw away string. Then there was a Kamante Islander called John (it was short for something), who was alleged to be fluent in any of the dialects likely to be used by the Mugus. John was well over six feet tall, and very hungry. He also indulged in gruesome daydreams; he once confided to me that he wished his great-grandparents had been cannibals, so that he could have something to boast about around the camp-fire, like the white members of the party. I was the fifth member, and as a comparative beginner in the adventure business my duties were humdrum enough. They included seeing that nobody got lost, finding them if they did, reminding Mrs Dyson when it was time for her medicine, fending off wild animals, helping Mr Bothe to fasten his guy-ropes, taking notes about anything that seemed odd, and dealing with the daily list of complaints from the native bearers. As I believe Vasco da Gama once observed, *somebody* has to boil the cabbage, even in the middle of an epic.

The place where the Mugus live turned

out to be so nearly inaccessible that I wondered at first why they didn't all go out of their minds.* We found them in a narrow cleft in the hills, four-thousand feet above sea level, hemmed in on three sides by densely wooded slopes, with an active volcano to the north, a haunted mountain to the east, three days of rain in a year, a week's tortuous journey to the coastal plain, and nothing to do when they got there.

For the last five miles old Mr Rossiter was carried by the native bearers. (They liked nothing better than carrying Mr Rossiter, because they got time and a quarter for it. Often they would snatch him up when no-one was looking and carry him, despite his protests, until they had earned enough for another booze-up when they got home, or until I happened to spot them, whichever was the sooner.) The rest of us managed to make it on foot, but we were in such bad shape when we finally reached the Mugu settlement that before we could even introduce ourselves we had to be rushed into the ju-ju house for treatment. There little men with *dumbali* feathers in their hair rubbed our feet with some kind of dirt, let a bit of our blood, and chanted incantations until we just couldn't bear it any longer, so we said we felt fine. I have often thought since that it was something of a triumph for witchcraft.

The average height of a Mugu is five foot five. (They smoke a good deal.) They speak a kind of bastard *D'hoi*, with a few words of Helianthemum and more than a trace of Poinsettia, so that John was able to translate for us without much difficulty. They were also adept at making themselves understood by signs. At any rate I *hope* they were, because otherwise much of the information we brought back is not going to be worth a row of beans. The chief was a hundred and eight. He had been elected because everybody owed him so much money.† It was either that or cut him up in pieces, so the

tossed for it. He had no teeth. He said white people had never been seen on the island before, although the Mugu had long suspected that such creatures might exist. One of their traditional songs, indeed, contains the lines:

Then cream-visaged strangers
With one wife each and haughty manners
Came out of the sea to befriend us.
O! Ah! O! Ah! O!

The chief expressed great interest in our wristwatches, our descriptions of life in Streatham, and our garments. (For all I know to the contrary he is still wearing the Jacqmar scarf that Mrs Dyson gave him in exchange for a couple of rubies, and in the same unconventional place.) He said he would be delighted to put us up if we wouldn't mind sharing a hut with thirty-eight other people. And so we began our life with the aborigines.

From July to October we tasted their primitive existence, studying their culture, technology, hats, mortuary customs, folklore, methods of crop rotation, adult education schemes, sculpture, garbage disposal, and political economy; and when we'd finished Mrs Dyson said she was very sorry but she didn't reckon much to them at all.

She exaggerated, of course. The life of the Mugu had a simplicity which I found enchanting, although I'm bound to say that forty-three people in a hut sixty yards long is a mistake. The hour before the evening meal, for example, was apt to be tedious, what with the wives deep-frying grass and rabbits in the communal pot, the men piling the children in a corner and sluicing them down with buckets of water, Mrs Dyson snoring in her hammock with a Chanel-soaked handkerchief over her face, old Mr Rossiter crawling about measuring people's skulls with a pair of calipers and crying out

† The Mugu are inveterate gamblers. Their favourite game, played with three pieces of wood on which faces have been engraved with red-hot sticks, is called Find the She-goat.

* I subsequently learned that seven of them had.

'Brachycephalic!' or 'Dolichocephalic!' in his piping voice, Mr Bothe being taught the steps of some ritual dance by a crowd of giggling grandmothers, and the teenagers daubing one another with a mixture of river-sand and fish-glue in readiness for some festival or other. The sleeping arrangements too, were far from satisfactory, because there were always revellers who came in late and walked on people, singing the good old songs and drinking out of bamboo hip-flasks. Some nights there would be a rumbling noise in the hills and Mrs Dyson would jump out of her hammock crying 'There goes that damn volcano again!' Then she would hustle everybody out into the darkness and stampede them into the forest to escape the creeping horror of an avalanche of molten lava. Everyone in the hut resented this, because it was well known that there was never more than a trickle of lava, and it always went the other way. The native bearers refused to sleep in the hut at any price, explaining that they preferred to make their own arrangements if it was all the same to us. I'm not sure what it is about native bearers, but they always seem to know what's good for them, and you'll never find one short of a couple of pounds to send home to his mother at the week-end.

But what are a few petty discomforts compared with the thrill of uncovering the secrets of a people who could trace their descent in an unbroken line right back to the Stone Age if they only put their minds to it? Helping to investigate the Mugu was one of the most rewarding experiences of my life, for it showed me the mockery of our so-called civilization. Here we are, riddled with guilt and dread and nervous indigestion in the midst of our clutter of spin-dryers, off-white telephones, double-action corn-flakes, electronic computers and quick-frozen chips: and all the time the Mugu are squatting in their impregnable valley, crudely fashioning axes and not even caring a hoot what day of the week it is, unless they happen to be next on the list for sacrifice to Ko, the volcano goddess. For they are essentially a happy people, if slightly stupid. The sound of their merry laughter comes back to me now* as I think of them hitting one another on the head with slabs of alabaster in the midsummer mating game, or lying in hot cinders to cure their dandruff, or kicking their spare wives into the river in an intriguing ceremony of great antiquity (the ones that float are taken out and put up for auction), or chewing the traditional live fresh-water fish on someone's birthday, or gathering poisonous berries in the woods in the cool of the morning, or shredding them into a friend's midday stew to settle a difference of opinion. No worries here about super-tax or corked claret, no frustrations about parking, no dissatisfaction with the quality of the caviar on long-distance flights, no fear of your ball-point pen leaking all over your drip-dry shirt, no sleepless nights over stocks and shares or what to wear if it happens to rain in Venice. How I envied them! Here at last, I thought, was the idyllic, uncomplicated life for which all men had yearned for years in secret, and these delightful Mugu took it all for granted!

We played their simple games. We ate their parboiled mice, cold insect soup, braised fillets of wolf, seagulls' eyes in batter, and other homely dishes. (The Mugu didn't like any of them much, which seems strange.) We fought alongside them at their weddings, coming-out parties and propitiation ceremonies. With the exception of Mr Rossiter, who said it wasn't his department, we attended several orgies, sitting in a kind of minstrels' gallery as honoured guests and helping to bury the dead the next morning. We studied their typically uncomplicated national ailments, such as asthma, dropsy, eye-sores, hereditary deafness, alcoholism, trench mouth, colour-blindness, epilepsy, myopia, eczema, premature senility and a

_____

* It is really a sort of uncontrollable giggle.

tendency to shrink in hot water. (I should point out that, at any given time, one Mugu in thirty is not attending the witch-doctor. Average expectation of life is seven years. The only thing they have a cure for is measles, and hardly any of them get it.) We studied their demonstrations of religious fervour, those who worship the volcano chasing those who worship the haunted mountain up trees and chopping off their arms with hatchets. We noted that they have no proper clothes, no industries, no sense of moral values, no future, no democracy, no potatoes, no stamina, no fuel, no shame, and no hope. They are there and that is all, and they sing some very peculiar songs.

I could not but wonder on the last day of our visit, as we crawled painfully aboard the landing-craft and set our course for home, whether the time will ever come when the rest of the world manages to catch up with the Mugu. I remember I asked one of the native bearers, and he said 'Brother, I shouldn't worry one bit if I were you. The way you're going you'll equal them in no time at all.'

1.6.1960

'This is a message from the great white Queen across the big water, to her loyal subjects of the M'Bongi tribe: "Keep on trucking" …'

'It appears they make their own necklaces from Coke can ring-pulls.'

'He says he'll swap you a ditigal watch for your beads.'

'He asks why "Mungo" has gone out of fashion as
a Christian name . . .'

'I'm afraid you'll have to
stop the bus – Mrs Scully
needs the lavatory again.'

Jo Packer

RED SHADOW IN REVERSE

Anyone who has seen both *The Desert Song* and the real hash-growing Riff Mountains knows that Red Shadow couldn't have been banished into the desert as neatly and conveniently as the stage setting always shows. At least two days' journey lies between the rocky hideouts and the sand, most of it across a very fertile belt. Do we view John Hanson tripping over grape vines and tramping through fields of tomatoes? No; but it happens.

It happened to me when I made my way up from El Golea in central Algeria to Tangier in northern Morocco. I had reached the desert by charter flight, and my fellow-passengers, all farmers, doctors and heating engineers, who were to do a luxury double crossing of the Sahara, left in Land Rovers as soon as we arrived, the springs of the vehicles reversed through the weight of the tins of herring roes aboard.

I hung around in El Golea for a day in order to make an honest penny, because I had managed to get on the trip only by promising my husband that I would not use any of our travel allowance. I went down to the market with a box of old clothes, jewellery and children's toys filched from my own flesh and blood while he was asleep.

However, it wasn't a bit like matriarchal Sneinton Market in Nottingham; in fact in the whole of Allah's little acre there wasn't a woman to be seen, either buying or selling. I recoiled with culture shock, took my load back to the hotel and set up Jo's Junkery in the yard. The waiter, the barman and the

sweeper soon flocked to the spot, and within a few minutes I had a clutter-free home in Surrey and about £8 in Algerian dinars.

Next morning at dawn I trudged out to the edge of the oasis and stood beside a signpost which pointed in two directions: north and south. 'Waited 48 hours for a lift to In Salah,' said a scratched message on the southern half, and since I am not one who yearns to beat buried-alive-in-the-sand sort of records, it prompted me to jump aboard the first lorry that stopped.

As we went along the driver told me in French that he was following the road northwards for only ten kilometres, then intended to turn off across the desert to pick up something from a construction project. He suggested I stay with him and leave when we regained the road. I agreed because the lure of a possible atomic reactor built with Russian aid and hidden behind the dunes was too strong.

But the Kremlin knows how to choose its crackpot drivers. After going over the desert for a mile my companion asked: 'Have you made love to any Algerians yet?' and when I replied no he began to wave his free hand reprovingly and cry out aloud about my unkindness to his fellow-countrymen. I had heard the same from some road-builders in my hotel and didn't want to go through the pros and cons again, especially in French, so I threatened: 'If you don't change the subject I'll get out.'

'Get out then!' the driver said, stopping the lorry. By the time I had descended and pulled out my three pieces of baggage he had relented, but I had not. 'Je marche,' I said, and began to do a Charlie Chaplin, weighed over at one side by a rolled sleeping-bag containing fossils, oranges and face cream.

As soon as the lorry had pulled away I very quickly dropped the dramatics because I realised I couldn't see the road and had no idea where it lay. The wind, which blows for ninety-four gritty per cent of the time in the Sahara, had whipped away the tyre marks and transferred the sand into my shopping bag.

At last I saw a black hyphen near the horizon and it turned out to be my next lift. A long camion, which had been on the move for the last fortnight, it had stopped for mint tea break at the side of the road. Six passengers, picked up from various points north of Nigeria, had practically set up house inside the sacks of the load.

The driver, a huge black Sudanese, and the mechanic, a little Arab, had a seesaw kind of relationship. In the cab the driver was boss, wit and raconteur, while on the ground the mechanic took over these roles as best he could. When I asked if I could photograph them the man from Sudan put his head up in a noble pose but the Arab turned his away, saying that his face 'wasn't good enough.' After we had divebombed down to our destination in the Valley of the M'zabites that afternoon they charged me 15/- for 150 miles; fair enough, since I knew that to use the infrequent taxi service with six or seven other passengers would have cost me £1. In fact, had it been Britain they might have got a commendatory scroll from the Prices and Incomes Board.

Outside the town of Ghardaia I was almost immediately picked up again by two young Army officers in an Opel, who drove towards Oran as though they had a date with a coup at midnight. They made exotic bedouins spring away from their tyres like so many sprays of mud, and kept the speedo at eighty past the last pile of sand, though I felt I ought to roll in it and whip myself with tamarisk twigs to ensure my return.

While daylight lasted my military friends were pleasant and sentimental boys, but when night fell they came over all queer. Stopping for a drink at a huge hotel near some grottoes, one of them displayed his prowess at Arab-philosophies-set-to-music while the other talked to me, but neither took the slightest notice of a tame deer which was ruining the fabulous carpet under our very

feet. A third man joined us, and after I had exchanged a few pleasantries with him my own gallant jumped up with the words: 'You're no good! You must go!'

I agreed, relieved rather than peeved, shook hands all round and resumed the open road. I had only gone a few yards when I found that the third man was in my wake, inviting me with many gracious gestures to get into his car so that he could take me 'wherever I wanted.' As I settled myself in the front seat the officer came plunging out of the hotel and started to argue with my benefactor, even trying to tighten the knot of his terylene tie. They must have reached an agreement because I was then asked to return to my former seat in the Opel. I did so, and the men went back into the hotel with their arms round each other's waists.

After ten minutes' wait I began to wonder why I was sitting there like a statue of a gooseberry. Leaving the car, I hid in a cave. When the men emerged they made a great show of roaring up and down the road with headlamps full on but didn't bother to search the rock formation, thinking no doubt that it was just a lot of elfin grot.

During the long tramp into Oran I tried to live off the land until I realised, after several fumbles in wayside fields had proved fruitless, that it was winter.

On the outskirts of the city I knew that I could now proceed by public transport, and asked two men in a van the way to the station. They offered to take me there but told me en route that there would be no train to the Moroccan border till the next morning. 'Come and stay at our house,' they said, for they seemed to be either cousins or brothers. 'We'll go to the station at dawn,'

The house was a large economy family size, probably with several people abed behind each closed door. My escorts led me into a huge chamber and left me alone.

Someone had been studying French history at school, for the room was done out like a corner of Versailles. A full-scale chandelier hung over the Sun King double bed, while ormolu wall-lamps and teak-finish tables twinkled away on either side. The wardrobe occupied nearly a whole wall, and the glass dressing-table would have taken Marie Antoinette and two maids very comfortably. Two decanters full of red and green water stood in front of the wing mirrors. I missed the portraits, but felt I couldn't moan about that in a Muslim house-hold.

I had just put on my sleeping-sweater and pyjama trousers when there was a quick tap at the door. The younger of the two men walked in and began to undress without a word.

'What?' I said. 'I can't sleep with you; I'm married.'

It was the easiest chop ever. The boy put on his djelaba again as a dressing-gown, said: 'So your husband is the lucky man, alors!' and even shook hands before departing. I smirked after him, thinking what a nice clean-living lad he was.

'It wasn't until I spent my summer holidays in London that I felt the urge to put anything aside for a rainy day.'

When number two entered the room I could see straight away that he was a different dose of cheeky chappie mixture. His long grim face and long grimy drawers had no right beneath chandelier light, I felt; he was like a Smarties-eater at La Scala, Milan. However, he had an unchallengeable entry ticket. 'This is my bedroom,' he said, in reply to my no-fratting plea. 'My wife has just gone away to visit relatives; if I don't sleep here, where shall I sleep?'

I couldn't think of an answer. I solved the dilemma by unrolling my sleeping-bag over a gold lamé mat on the floor. This displeased him but he didn't try to drag me up to his level. He threw a pillow down and soon fell asleep.

When his alarm clock went off at six am he silenced it and slept again. I got dressed, then tapped him on the shoulder. He leapt up, saying we must hurry. When we reached the front door he mumbled: 'Can't drive you to the station – no petrol – au revoir,' and closed the wooden keep behind me.

I stood in the street for a minute or two, translating his French, then flew into a rage and beat on the door, screaming. He was back again like a shot, still in his drawers. Though he offered to get dressed and take me to the station, I was by that time satisfied. His family and neighbours knew that jig-gery-pokery had been going on with an infidel, and if they didn't the many workmen going up the street would soon tell them. I tried to put a wiggle in my stalk as I departed.

I got a bus to the station and a train soon after. I could relax, for I still had half of my dinars left, and a husband and working holiday awaited me in Morocco. As we trav-elled along the base of the Riff Mountains late that afternoon, I found I had one worry. I was thinking of the crimson-caped crusader and humming 'The Desert Song' and 'Song of the Riff' alternately. The geographical error of the whole banishment scene at the Cambridge Theatre began to bother me. Eventually I decided that the two-day gap 'twixt rocks and sand had been omitted entirely because it would have slowed the story and ruined the romance, with Red Shadow running in and out of woman trouble like patches of fog all the way down.

31.7.1968

'How can I be sure the money will reach the snake?'

A. P. Herbert

THE CHARM OF ALGIERS

'*Panorame!*' said the taxi-driver, and drew up on the cliff's edge. '*Grand panorame!*' said the taxi-driver, and waved his hand towards the rain-swept sea. '*Panorame!*' said the taxi-driver, and pointed proudly downwards to the warehouse roofs.

It was to see this *panorame* that the genial Algerian had driven us two miles out of our way in defiance of orders and at about twenty francs a second. There is no escaping this 'superb view.' You may shout till you are speechless that you wish to return to the ship, that you wish to drive in the opposite direction, that you wish to get out; but sooner or later your taxi will find its way to this spot and the patriotic Frenchman (of Arab-Maltese-Levantine extraction) will proudly say, '*Grand panorame!*'

And personally I never have the heart to

express my profound dissatisfaction with the view. I have now seen it four times. Three times it was raining. But it is perhaps a view which looks its best in the driving rain. When it is not raining you can see a long way from this spot; and to guides and tourist agencies, and, alas! to most of us poor tourists, whenever it is possible to see a long way, that is a 'view,' and it matters little what particular objects are visible. To me, however, vile Philistine, this matters greatly. From this spot, I repeat, you can see a lot of Algiers, a lot of warehouses, hotels, lodging-houses and villas, two mosques and large quantities of the sea. There is generally something to be said for the sea. But nobody can really want to look for long at a lot of Algiers, unless he has paid money to cross the seas and look at Algiers and is determined to get his money's worth.

Such a one will endear himself to the Algerian taxi-driver, and I wish them both good fortune. But personally I would just as soon stand in the rain on Campden Hill and look down on Kensington or Notting Dale. The 'view' in both directions is extensive and therefore 'superb'; and if they were on the north coast of Africa these views would definitely count as 'panorames.' The roofs of Algiers are cleaner, it is true, but on the whole they are much more modern and just as dull; though here and there a post-office, bank or municipal building of Moorish design gives the untravelled visitor a thrilling sense of the immemorial East.

I cannot say very much more for the superb view of Algiers as you approach it from the sea. This has always reminded me of Hastings, and I suppose it always will. Certainly the 'front,' with its long line of rectangular 'blocks,' solid hotels and offices and shops, is pure Hastings. And very nice too. On the other hand, it is perhaps a disappointing introduction to the mystery of Africa.

Yet everybody bounded out of their bunks this morning to catch the first glimpse of the celebrated Algiers. I came up a little later and saw a large black gasometer and two tall factory chimneys standing nobly on the very shore of the Muddyterranean. In the driving rain they had a sort of wistful beauty which is not attained by the gasometers of England.

At lunch-time, true, the sun shone gloriously for half-an-hour, and up at the fine hotel on the hill one sat under the palms and looked at the gorgeous flowers of Africa – nasturtiums and roses, cyclamen and stocks. And after lunch, wandering through the garden in the rain, we had an intimate contact with Oriental life – two French ladies in *yashmaks* and Arab dress collecting money for a charity (unnamed).

I would not discourage anyone from the pilgrimage to Algiers. They tell me the African sun shines there; I only know that in my experience three times out of four the African drizzle is at work. But no doubt I have visited the place at the wrong time of the year. I find that I generally do go to places at the wrong time of the year. Invalids, I believe, survive at Algiers for quite a long time. And, tucked away in a corner of this large French town, there is a genuine and insanitary Arab quarter, where many of the Arabs, I should say, have pure Arab blood in them. And there are gentlemen in the *fez*, *tarboosh*, or what-is-it, walking thrillingly about the wide French streets. Imagine the thrill, brothers, if you saw an Arab (with *fez* or *yashmak*) in the streets of Hastings – on the Leas at Folkestone!

That is really the point. Are we making enough of our English Algerias? The excellent spring 'cruises' of our steamship companies are a great success (I should make it clear, perhaps, that the good ship *Orange* is visiting many places more satisfying and stimulating than Algiers); but what about the summer months when the South is too hot? Why no cruises round the fair coast of England? Say that the good ship *Orange* anchors off Folkestone, off Brighton, off Blackpool. Imagine the tourists – French,

American, German (and even British) – crowding ashore to see the beauties of the land and the queer life of the 'natives.' 'Expeditions' into the interior – Sussex villages, the Downs (which can knock spots off the Atlas Mountains), the wild tribes of Cornwall and Lancashire. A special trip, of course, to see the Furry Dance of Helston, which, I am confident, is far more strange and exciting than the drivelling exhibitions of any brown and black men. I have suffered 'native' dances all over the world, and never saw anything worth looking at, except the Maoris. Dash it! why not a village of Ancient Britons? They would be at least as genuine as the Arabs of Algiers. Algiers is only a French town with an Arab slum at one end. Well, England has a slum or two and a foreign quarter or two. Only we don't attempt to persuade the foreigner that he ought to sail across the seas to see them. Algiers has nothing –

No, I am wrong. Algiers *has* something. She has an absence of ridiculous laws, regulations, restrictions, Watch Committees, *et hoc genus omne*. You can drink her somewhat dreary wines whenever you wish to; you can go to the Casino and recklessly gamble away ten shillings without becoming amenable to the law; and the people whose business it is to entertain or refresh you are not harried by magistrates or spied on by policemen. Algiers, with all its defects, is civilised; our British counterparts, with all their attractions, are mediævally or barbarously governed. But never mind, in a British ship at least the Briton can still be free, buy beer when he likes, and even enter for a wicked sweepstake on the Derby. The British liner is not, as the lawyers have it, a floating bit of Britain, but, Heaven be praised! a floating bit of the Continent. So he who goes upon these 'cruises' of mine will be able to see England by day and sleep abroad. And if I had a liner or two I should get busy at once.

13.4.1932

Michael Bywater

GIDDY GOAT

The dead goat may have had something to do with it, but I found myself thinking about sex a lot. A great deal. And in a surprisingly dismal fashion. None of this stuff you usually get when you think about sex: 'Gosh, I'm thinking about sex,' and then, after a bit, 'Ha ha, sex, whoopee.' More in the manner I imagine a bivalve would think about sex: a long gloomy blank, a feeling of time dripping slowly and irrecoverably past, and then, 'What is it all about? What is it all about? What is it all about?' followed by torpor and indolence, drifting morosely in the current, the two halves of the shell occasionally creaking open to admit a dose of delicious sewage.

Or, in my case, goat.

A Moroccan goat, this one, slightly dead when we found it, some miles outside Temara on a hillside sloping down to the ocean, lying on its side with its snout tucked up against a hoof as though it was trying to sniff out whether it had trodden in something and had died of depression in the process. It was a cruel trick on God's part to deprive goats of the ability to die with dignity. Nothing looks more feeble and pointless than a dead goat, unless it's the debris of the multiple car/camel-crashes which you can see any day on the road between Abu Dhabi and Bahrein; or possibly also a dead starfish, a curiosity so lacking in gravity and pith that you might well become a saint or prophet if you stared at one long enough.

It was also somewhat sodden, giving off that peculiar smell of wet goat which is also the smell of dead goat; which must make it depressing for live goats in the wet weather. Perhaps there's some sort of evolutionary ancestral memory there, perhaps that's why we still think of death when it rains, except that, as I said, I was thinking about sex; and there's no connection between the smell of dead wet goat and sex, that I *do* know; or at any rate, there shouldn't be.

Mustapha and the brother saw it first, which was fitting, as it was their goat.

– Dead goat, said the brother.

– Dinner *insh'*-Allah, said Mustapha.

I sloshed over and prodded it with my desert boot. It was definitely dead.

– No, no, said Mustapha, bending down and placing his head on the goat's heart, it's only slightly dying. If we kill it, it will be all right, *kif-kif*, same-same as butchery.

When a devout Muslim is prepared to compromise his eternal reward in order to give one a dead goat dinner, the least a White Man can do is look flattered. It is slightly hard to look suitably honoured when one's flatterer is lying with his head in a dead goat's armpit, talking through a mouthful of sodden fur, but I managed it. The sight itself left me relatively unmoved; only a few hours beforehand I had seen the brother with *his* head poked up the neck of a severed cow-head, blowing hard, while another brother (three down, seventeen to go) bashed the cow-head with a large stick. I took a photograph of this example of Mussulman *charcuterie*, which caused annoyance, and annoyance is something one doesn't cause before an open-air abattoir staffed by young men with sharp knives, already drenched in blood so that a little more will do no harm.

Being annoyed, they advanced, with their knives. The brother pulled his head from the cow's, with a little wet 'plop' which made even my hardened stomach twitch, and shouted, in a rather bubbling damp voice: 'La! La! Sadiq! Friend!' The hordes got the point, that I was to be regarded as one of them for the purposes of the debate, so paused, put their knives down, and then started coming at me again. Honour would not permit them to stab me like an infidel; they would beat me to death like a brother.

But I escaped, and now it was raining, and Mustapha, with his head, as aforesaid, in a dead goat's armpit in the rain, was honouring me by swearing that it *wasn't* dead and so could be killed in the correct manner, which he did by cutting its throat.

WEEDY COWARDLY READERS SKIP THE NEXT PARAGRAPH.

The blood should gush out, really, but we didn't wait to find out. We strolled a few yards away and looked deliberately out to sea.

– Tell that prayer again, said the brother. It is good.

This was my prayer which had made it rain, alleviating the four-year drought. That morning, Mustapha had told me that the King of Morocco had ordered the entire nation to pray for rain, but without effect. 'This is not a problem for you,' he asserted. 'It certainly is,' I said. 'Do you pray? Have you prayers like us?'

I reached for the good old Missal. *Oratio ad petendam pluviam*. No trouble. '*Deus in quo vivimus movemur et sumus, pluviae nobis tribue congregemur,*' and so on.

'Russian?' said the brother.

'No, Latin.'

'Ah yes. Like they spoke in Greece.'

Three hours later it began to rain, and now we were on the hillside preparing for a feast of illegally already-dead goat. To pass the time while the goat exsanguinated, or not, we discussed theology and contemporary *mores*.

– Your God made it rain also.

– Yes.

– But he's same-same, *kif-kif* as Allah. Only one God.

– Yes.

– But I heard they have people in England–America who do not believe.

– That is so.

– And they *say* this? In the streets? In the newspapers?

– Yes.

– But you have prayers.

– Yes, but they do not use them.

– What do they do, then?

– Appoint a person called Mr Howell.

– Bloody ju-ju. I understand. Ju-ju better than Allah, eh? This is very primitive. All like your people in England–America thinks of women only for the doings. That same reason.

– Doings?

– Doings. Only for doings. No respect or family or babies. No sons. All *kif-kif* like not believing in God.

– Or Allah.

– Same-same. Here we believe in Allah. It is obvious. I think the goat is now dead.

Which, of course, it was, and always had been.

– I think the rain has washed the blood away altogether, *insh'Allah*, said the brother.

We carried the goat up the hill to the house. After a mile, Mustapha spoke.

– Perhaps he was dead before. Perhaps we did not see.

– What about your religious laws?

– The feast is for you. It is your God who sees it.

– But you said Allah *kif-kif* as God.

– Evidently. But sometimes he wears a different pair of shoes.

It was after the goat supper that I began to think of sex, the prospect of sleep having receded forever in a fearsome bout of Allah's Revenge. The Berber girl sleeping in the next room in my otherwise-empty house was astonishingly beautiful, was not my wife, had made it quite clear that she had rapidly developed a great friendship for me, and I knew perfectly well that to lay a finger upon her was quite out of the question.

To tell the truth, I was relieved. If you need me to explain why, forget it.

Enough to say that all my brooding ruminations were amply confirmed when, on boarding the aeroplane home last week, I saw on the cover of the glossy women's magazine the girl next to me was 'reading', the banner headline HOW TO HAVE MUCH MORE SEX.

There's the modern England–American girl for you. All bloody *kif-kif* with dead goats, as far as I'm concerned.

18.1.1984

'It was a lovely little palm-treed oasis before the developers moved in.'

'So we thought, "What the hell, why not make a day of it!"'

'I'll tell you what we've discovered – we've discovered that you need your eyes tested!'

"Would you care to see the
English Quarter, señor?"

'The wife and I had a holiday here once, before the war. Course, we didn't have the tank with us that time.'

*'Frank thought he'd put one over on the Arabs by shoplifting in **their** country.'*

H. F. Ellis

FROM MY TRAVEL BOOK

The sultan received me in the embroidered tent he uses as a throne room. He is tall for a sultan and has the dignity and perfect manners of his race.

'Would you prefer the brailings up or down?' he asked me, as soon as I had taken my seat on the low *pouffe* at his side. The sun was striking down with tropical heat and the atmosphere inside the little tent was stifling. Steam rose in fitful puffs from the bowl of rose water by my side.

I asked that the brailings might be raised, but noticing that they were already up, changed my mind and begged that they should be lowered. The Sultan inclined his head and motioned to a gigantic Nubian to leave them as they were. In his country, as I should have remembered, politeness demands that the guest ask always for the opposite of what he desires. Ignorance of this interesting custom has sometimes cost an unwary visitor dear.

'And your wives?' he inquired. 'I trust they bloom like the lily of the valley and wax fat as kine by the water-meadows of Yemen.'

I said yes, that apart from a mild epidemic of measles in one of the dormitories, they were all well at home. Though himself monogamous, the Sultan naturally assumes that any guest of his has great possessions, and it would be discourteous to correct him.

'And the sultana?' I asked boldly. 'May I hope that no one has had the audacity to cut *her* currant off?'

The Sultan enjoys a joke, as I well knew,

better than most men, but the reader must remember that we were conversing in Arabic and for a moment there was a baffled look in his fine, rather un-English eyes.

'In my country,' I explained, 'the power that flows along the pipes to bring heat and light to our houses is at times cut off –'

'How cut off?' he asked. 'By the sword?'

I sought about in my mind for the Arabic for 'switch'.

'There is a handle,' I said. 'It is because there is a scarcity of the lumps of compressed vegetable-matter we dig up and burn to make the power that flows along the pipes.'

'Here in this land,' he said, 'we do not dig vegetables from the ground to burn. That would be accounted a sin. My herd of four thousand camels –'

'These are very old vegetables,' I said hastily, 'buried many hundreds of cubits beneath the ground.'

'The ways of Allah are strange,' he said gravely. 'But the ways of men pass all understanding. Let us eat.'

He clapped his hands and at once the customary whole boiled sheep, swimming in its cauldron of fat, was set before each of us. For some hours there was silence as we ate, but at last I threw the final bone back with a clatter into the empty cauldron and turned my streaming face to the Sultan.

'So,' I said. 'The jackals of hunger have been put to flight. Let us talk.'

'Good!' said the sultan. 'But first – you will have another?'

'No, thank you,' I replied – and could have bitten out my tongue when I realised my error and a second sheep was set before me. To have refused to eat it now would have been, in my host's eyes, a bitter insult, but it was, I confess, with some nausea that I fished up a forequarter and once more set my teeth in the scalding flesh. And when, just after sunset, I pushed the cauldron away and dipped my fingers in the rose bowl to signify repletion, the head and portions of the scrag-end still remained untasted.

'How then?' said the Sultan, frowning. 'It is not to your liking?'

'It is excellent,' I said, repressing a shudder. 'But in my country there is a saying "Enough is as good as a feast."'

'It is true,' he said. 'But we have not feasted. To-night, if Allah wills, we shall feast – I and my brethren and my brethren-in-law and the husbands of my daughters and you, who are dearer to me than the father of my own sons. Be sure the feast will be as good as enough. Many sheep have been slaughtered in your honour.'

'Your bountiful kindness,' I replied desperately, 'is sweeter to me than honey to the sweet-toothed Ethiopian. But in my country it is not the custom to eat the flesh of the sheep a second time before the sun has thrice completed the great circle of the heavens and returned again to his appointed place. The hindquarters of a single lamb is the portion that is set apart among my people for four persons to feast upon, here a little and there a little, until the space of seven days has passed by.'

The Sultan expressed his astonishment. 'The customs of one people are not those of another,' he remarked courteously; and he gave immediate orders that two score goats and a hundred doves be broiled for the feast. 'The flesh of the goat is not the flesh of the sheep,' he pointed out.

But it was not until we strolled out together for a breather before the evening meal that I realised how boundless is the hospitality of the people of this forgotten corner of Arabia. Thick clouds of black smoke rolled across the velvety night sky and the air was heavy with the acrid smell of autumn bonfires. 'They are burning old vegetables,' explained my host, 'to make hot the flesh of the goat. There is a saying among my people, "The customs of the stranger are our customs."'

I hardly knew how to thank him.

15.1.1947

LET ME THROUGH I'M A TOURIST!

HONEYSETT joins the swarm of foreign visitors packed into London

'Would you like to see the waiting list, sir?'

'You didn't say anything about sharing.'

'There are two more imposters in 703, Mr Dunmore.'

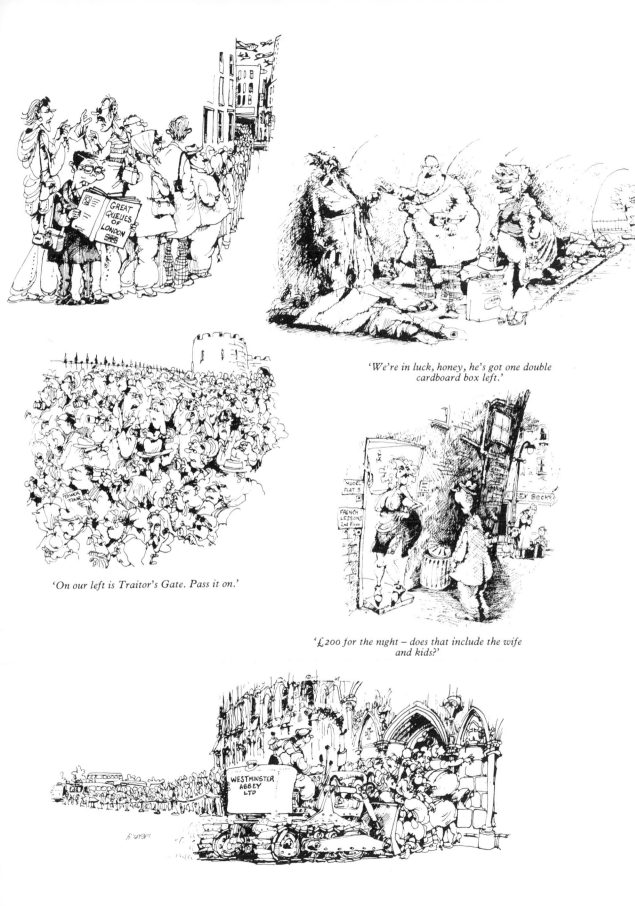

'We're in luck, honey, he's got one double cardboard box left.'

'On our left is Traitor's Gate. Pass it on.'

'£200 for the night – does that include the wife and kids?'

GREAT QUEUES OF LONDON

WESTMINSTER ABBEY LTD

'Somebody's Daddy obviously didn't keep
up the maintenance payments.'

SINGLES PLEASE
MERRILY HARPUR's
one-parent family holiday

'I'm bringing them with me in the hope
that they'll be brought up by wolves.'

'Make it single cream – that'll really annoy him.'

'He identifies with the sausages.'

'Put it to your ear and you'll hear the faraway
hissing of your father.'

'No, that's Mr and **Miss** Smith . . .'

David Taylor

THE PUNCH TRANS-ATLANTIC ENDURANCE CUP

13 Days, 8 hours, 44 minutes and 12 seconds – a shattering new world record!

Chief Pilot of 'British' confirms:

IT'S THE FASTEST-EVER CROSS-ING AT THE LOWEST-EVER FARE

Stand-by passenger queues for nearly a fortnight but save £££s on regular ticket

'Knackered, but over the moon!'

That was the scarcely-audible croak of triumph from an exhausted and ashen-faced former lone round-the-world yachtsman, Eric Shackleton, today, as he staggered retching down the aircraft steps, keeled over to kiss the tarmac at New York airport – and became the first man in history to cross the Atlantic solo for just £59.99 inside a fortnight.

GRUELLING

First to fight a path through the hysterical crowds scrambling to board the epoch-making plane on the off chance of a cut-price return flight was Eric's travel agent, coach and wife, Dame Nellie Shackleton, the veteran off-peak lady aviator. She brought Eric the incredible news he had endured so long to hear – she has managed to fix him up with a Low Season Stand-By Super-ANTHRAX Pennysnatcher ticket on to Los Angeles – and he's wait-listed for a third leg over the pole to Hong Kong!

STAMINA

Months of meticulous planning for his marathon feat finally paid off for Eric when, despite an afternoon lost through road works on the M25 and a nasty backside injury sustained during the interminable days of sitting queuing at Gatwick – waiting, waiting for his name to be called, he realised after take-off that he was in with a chance of clipping more than 36 hours and £5.01 off the previous record set last Tuesday by French naval PT instructor, Serge Amundsen.

CHALLENGE

Now the international race is on to match Eric's heroic adventure westbound from Gatwick with a daring bid to conquer the great routes eastbound – where jet-lag can be a killer. But the prize is high – up to £299 off the regular ticket to Singapore on some Thursdays, *half-price* to Bangkok provided certain advance-booking conditions are met.

GOAL

Eric is non-committal about his future plans but is rumoured to be in hard training to take a crack at unemployed weight-lifter Pete 'Iron Biceps' Edmundsen's Luton to Java single-handed best of 12 days, 7 hours, 15 minutes and 31 seconds, for £79.99 *return* on a Shoulder Period Discount Affinity Group Special Offer Spouse Farebuster, including an unlimited mileage Simca or other fine car.

MY WORST MOMENTS
By Eric

'There were times when I came close to despair. After six days in the queue for a stand-by boarding pass, I broke down and asked a stewardess what it would cost to buy an ordinary ticket to New York. She collapsed laughing and, somehow, that seemed to bring me back to my senses and from somewhere I found the strength to hold on.

'I was airborne after only 12 days and thought my troubles were over. But when you are tired and wet and cold and hungry, the mind plays tricks on you. There were only six students and a rucksack occupying. my seat but even a little niggle like that, when there's hundreds of screaming kids on board, can get to you. I started to imagine all sorts of terrible things, like that they might start serving a "Taste of Olde England" buttered goose Sir Walter Raleigh with croquettes Ann Boleyn and a free flagon of mulled mead or make us all sit and read *High Life*. For a moment, I thought I was going to go under but I just kept thinking to myself what I'd be paying in First Class and, somehow, I managed to hold on.'

THE STRUGGLE JUST TO SURVIVE

How Eric managed to keep going through the long days

'Conditions in the cruel sea of people at Gatwick were the worst I've ever known. There was a tremendous swell every time the Solari chattered to announce some new departure, then there would be agonising periods when everything was becalmed. At times I felt terribly alone. No information,

Crisis on Day Two of the endurance trial. With no fresh victuals since he forced a passage into Gatwick Departures. Eric suffers agonising stomach cramps and must decide either to break in to his emergency supply of Banjo bars or risk putting the mission in peril . . .

no one to talk to, no means of knowing whether or not I'd ever arrive – the psychological tensions were every bit as bad as the physical hardships.

'I tried to keep my nerve by reading and re-reading the conditions of the Warsaw Convention printed inside my ticket. Now and again, I managed to snatch some troubled sleep on a plastic seat that was caked in sweat and the discarded remnants of individual fruit pies – a grim reminder that others before me had sought to conquer the seemingly overwhelming power of the seething waves of stand-by passengers, crashing relentlessly against the battered check-in desks.

'For six days and nights, I managed somehow to hold myself together on nothing but spam baps and ring-pull cans of 7-Up, not daring to touch my emergency supply of Banjo bars and a Thermos of Lucozade in case I should have to face a strike situation with the in-flight catering or, worse, being stacked over Boston or diverted to Gander where it is rumoured that so many who came before have perished.

'I think I reached the outer limits of human endurance on the coach out from the terminal to the plane – still I shut my eyes to think of it and can find no words which adequately express the squalor and degradation we suffered when two wide-bodied flights were combined because of staff sickness. Such was the anguish I then suffered, I clean forgot to take on duty-free supplies and put the whole adventure in jeopardy.

'I won't say that I'd do it again, yet I take pride in the fact that I accomplished my goal – it was perhaps the most exhilarating fortnight's holiday which any man can ask.'*

13.8.1980

*Extracted from *Alone I Did It*, Eric Shackleton's moving account of one man's battle against the elements of fortune, published by The Headstone Press, £9.95 or free when you book a three-week holiday of your dreams on Baffin Island.

Safety margins are pushed to the limit as Eric and fellow competitors jostle for a good position on the starting line. Officials described conditions as 'treacherous' and warned that those setting out across the ocean without proper preparation risked being lost for ever in a mountainous sea of people . . .

Alan Coren

TRUE SNAILS READ? (anag.)

Squire **Walt Reeny**, Dr **Yesvile**, and the rest of these gentlemen having asked me to write down the whole particulars about **True Snails Read?** from the beginning to the end, keeping nothing back but the answers to 14 across and 23 down, and that only because there is treasure still to be lifted, I take up my pen in the year of grace

17--, and go back to the time when my father kept the Admiral Benbow inn, and the brown old seaman with the terrible nib-scar first took up his lodging under our roof.

I remember him as if it were yesterday, as he came plodding to the inn door, his twenty-four salt-caked volumes of the *Oxford English Dictionary* following behind him in a hand-barrow, his high reedy voice breaking out in that old sea-song that was to haunt my dreams:

'Corpse at bottom of scrum! We hear

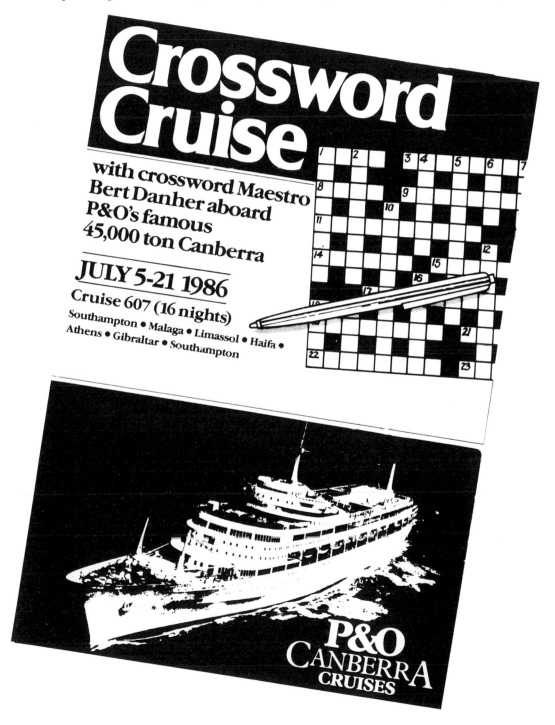

He's worth more than one small bier!'

I opened the door to him, and he threw himself into a chair, crying:

'A palindrome? Yes, but this one's not for kids, me hearties! It's peculiar.'

I stared at him.

'I beg your pardon, sir?' I said.

'I think,' said my father, from the dark recess of the bar, 'he wants a tot. Of, if I am not mistaken, rum.'

The stranger smote the table.

'Be 'ee a crosswordin' man?' he cried joyously.

My father smiled.

'4, 4, 1, 4,' he replied, **'according to the best fairy stories. Not these days, though.'**

The old sailor nodded, and, when my father went out for the bottle, drew me to him with an inky claw, so close that I could see the flecks of chewed quill stuck upon his lip, and smell the indiarubber on his nails.

'Yonder,' he whispered excitedly, nodding towards the bar-window and the broad bay beyond, 'lies the *S.S. Canberra*. I ships aboard 'er on the morrow tide.'

'You are bound for the Crossword Cruise, sir?' I exclaimed. 'You go in search of the Grand Prize? May I wish you the very best of luck?'

'Luck?' cried the old man in a terrible voice. **'Luck's a chance, but - - - - - - -'s sure (*Housman*) (7).** I makes my own luck, lad! See this 'ere diddy-box o' mine?'

I nodded. It was a battered, brassbound thing, with **FLAT CAP, INNIT?** engraved upon the lid.

'Yes,' I said, proud of myself, 'I noticed it immediately. It seemed such a queer shape for a hatbox.'

The old blood-threaded eyes gazed at me as if I were deranged.

'Hatbox?' he muttered. 'That be no hatbox, lad. That be the personal property o' the late –' and here his voice dropped to a cracked whisper '– *Captain Flint!*'

Letters swam in my head. Truth dawned.

'It be why I doan need luck, see?' said the old sailor. His eyes grew moist with more than rheum. 'Flint were the smartest puzzle dog I ever shipped with, lad. Flint knew the Latin handle of every plant that ever were, 'e 'ad the entire *Oxford Dictionary o' Quotes* to heart, 'e could spell backwards in fourteen lingos, 'e knew eight 'undred words wi' two letters in 'em! He dreamed in anagrams, did Flint, he saw acrostics in the stars. I remember one time we was becalmed off the Dry Tortegas, half-mad from heat and thirst and not a man among us capable o' getting 1 across in *The Sun* – It sat on the mat (3) – and there were Flint on the afterdeck, doing *The Telegraph* with 'is left hand and *The Times* with 'is right, while 'is parrot read him *The Guardian* so's he could do it in 'is head simultaneous!'

'Remarkable!' I cried.

'This rare genus had one eye (6),' murmured the old man, blowing his nose fiercely on a red bandanna, 'but has now **gone up to meet his dog (3).'**

'What, then, is in his box?' I enquired.

A dry hand closed over my own, so firmly that I could feel the sharp callus on a forefinger flattened by a million clues.

'Ye seems a lad who would **look after his short mother (4, 3),'** murmured the ancient. 'A year or two back, just after Flint 'ung up 'is sextant, the P&O come to 'im wi' a proposition. Not a sea-dog from Maracaibo to the Cape as 'adn't 'eard tell o' Flint's magic powers, see, an' it were only a matter o' course afore –'

'No need to go on, sir!' I cried. 'I may be a stranger to the cryptic force, but I can divine a drift as well as any! You are telling me that Flint became the brains behind the Crossword Cruise! You are intimating that the incalculable treasure which awaits one brilliant, albeit peculiar, passenger comes with the solution to a Grand Prize Jumbo Puzzle set by –'

My companion spread his hands, nodding.

'**Did the good doctor fail to diagnose his digestive problem? Sounds as though his friend Sherlock has! (10),**' he said.

I pointed excitedly at the diddy-box.

'And this can only mean,' I exclaimed, 'that you have Captain Flint's papers, and therefore the answer to the Canberra's Prize Jum –'

The finger was across my lips. Its tremble was so stricken that my ear-ring shook.

'*What is that strange tapping?*' he croaked.

I searched for the true meaning hidden in this cryptogram, knowing by now that *strange*, like *disturbed*, *confused*, *upset*, and so forth, betokened some anagrammatic interference. But what could I make from **tapping**? Was *gnippat* some rare Sumatran weevil, *pantpig* a Jacobean pervert, *Ignappt* the early working-title of something by that drunk Robert Louis Stevenson who lived in our small back room? It was while I was pondering this that I became aware of a noise beyond the window, as of a stick banging rhythmically against the wall.

I glanced at my companion, who had begun to gasp horribly.

'**We see nothing on this church bench! (5, 3),**' he managed, finally, to sob.

I swivelled as the inn door burst open; and caught my breath. At first, I saw naught but the white stick that had thrust it wide: but soon thereafter, a squat, malign figure entered the room, a dreadful leer playing beneath the sightless eyes. He tapped his way to our table, and, reaching out a clammy hand, touched my face.

'Pew,' he said. 'I am confused.'

Wep? I thought, *ewp?*

'I had been expecting an old friend, but – ah!' he cried, as his hand groped on and suddenly found my companion, cringing in his chair, 'I was not wrong.'

Whereupon he removed a folded scrap of paper from his smock, placed it carefully on the table between us, turned, and made his echoing way out again.

Since my companion seemed too stricken to move, I took the liberty of picking up the scrap and unfolding it. The eyes in the rigid face opposite now flickered in resigned enquiry.

'**Negro Topsy upside down? Don't say why! (5, 4),**' I read.

He groaned horribly. A further, deeper shudder racked his ancient frame. His eyes rolled to white. As a drowning man throws up one sinking hand, he beckoned me close.

'**Skin –**' he wheezed, but the rest of the sentence ebbed.

'Go on!' I urged. 'I could not hear!'

He made a supreme and dreadful effort.

'**Skin game – for Cricket Cup?**' he gasped, finally. '**(4, 3).**'

I racked such brain as I could muster. The ruin opposite, tongue lolling noiselessly behind cracked lips, could be no help.

And then, clouds parted, light burst through.

'Hide box!' I shouted.

He nodded, just perceptibly.

I snatched up Flint's precious bequest, wrapped it quickly in a tablecloth, rose, and would have left forthwith to seek a spot of suitable impenetrability, had not the dying unfortunate clutched at my urgent sleeve in one last desperate bid.

He pulled, with terminal strength, my ear towards his lip.

'Beware!'

His voice was like an on-shore breeze against the dry grass of the dunes.

'Beware of what?' I said.

The tongue laid a last bead of moisture on the lip.

'**Of a seafaring man with one backward ge!**' he gasped.

And died.

Next Week's Episode. **Hallmarked underwear? (4, 4, 6) Why not, if the parrot's good as gold! (6, 2, 5)**

2.7.1986

THESE FOOLISH THINGS

GRAHAM on holiday souvenirs

'It seems remarkably cheap for an original Picasso.'

'Do you do egg-cups?'

'Look, Annie – do we really want a goat-skin bedspread?'

'We went mad!'

'Here you are, Charles – you can sit on the camel saddle.'

'Three weeks ago that little lot was
tumbling over Thomson's Falls.'

'We're not very sure what it is, but it was hand-made by
local craftsmen.'

'What else did you bring back?'

Michael Heath

WATCH THIS
SPACE

**American tourists will be in space by the
year 2010**

Daily Telegraph

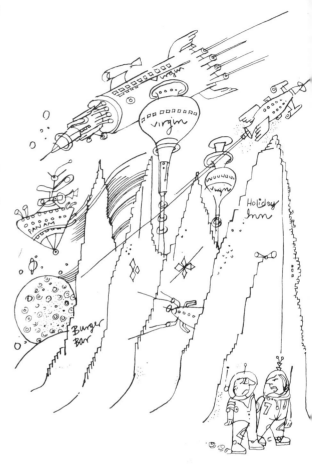

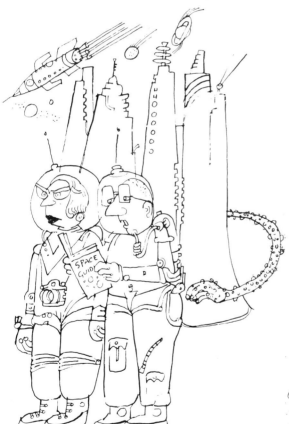

*'It says here we should beware of
local pickpockets.'*

*'Nine light years from home, and now you remember
that you forgot to turn off the gas.'*

'Well, at least it's safer here than in Europe.'

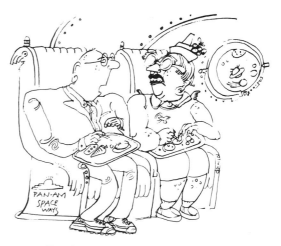

'I gather we may suffer a bit of turbulence
going through Star Wars.'

'The rest of our luggage either ended up in a black
hole or has been sent to planet Zong.'

'If you look out of the porthole you can see
Steven Spielberg's private planet.'

'I'm sorry, Bub, but I'm a stranger here myself.'